MCGRAW-HILL

Microsoft **PowerPoint** *97*

Timothy J. O'Leary
Arizona State University

Linda I. O'Leary

Irwin
McGraw-Hill

Boston, Massachusetts   Burr Ridge, Illinois   Dubuque, Iowa
Madison, Wisconsin   New York, New York   San Francisco, California   St. Louis, Missouri

Irwin/McGraw-Hill

A Division of The McGraw·Hill Companies

Microsoft PowerPoint 97

Copyright © 1998 by The McGraw-Hill Companies, Inc. All rights reserved. Printed in the United States of America. Except as permitted under the United States Copyright Act of 1976, no part of this publication may be reproduced or distributed in any form or by any means, or stored in a data base or retrieval system, without the prior written permission of the publisher.

This book is printed on acid-free paper.

domestic   3 4 5 6 7 8 9 0 BAN BAN 9 0 0 9
international   1 2 3 4 5 6 7 8 9 0 BAN BAN 9 0 0 9 8 7

ISBN 0-07-231669-1

The Sponsoring Editor was Rhonda Sands.
The Developmental Editor was Kristin Hepburn.
The Editorial Assistant was Kyle Thomes.
The Marketing Manager was James Rogers.
The Production Supervisor was Richard DeVitto.
The cover was designed by Lorna Lo.
Project management was by Elaine Brett, Fritz/Brett Associates.
Composition was by Pat Rogondino, Rogondino & Associates.
The typeface was ITC Clearface.
Banta Co. was the printer and binder.

Information has been obtained by The McGraw-Hill Companies, Inc. from sources believed to be reliable. However, because of the possibility of human or mechanical error by our sources, The McGraw-Hill Companies, Inc. or others, The McGraw-Hill Companies, Inc. does not guarantee the accuracy, adequacy, or completeness of any information and is not responsible for any errors or omissions or the results obtained from use of such information.

Library of Congress Cataloging Card Number 97-72179

International Edition
Copyright © 1998. Exclusive rights by The McGraw-Hill Companies, Inc., for manufacture and export. This book cannot be re-exported from the country to which it is consigned by The McGraw-Hill Companies, Inc. The International Edition is not available in North America.

When ordering this title, use ISBN 0-07-115476-0

http://www.mhhe.com

Contents

Graphics Presentation Program Overview

You are in a panic! Tomorrow you are to make a presentation and you want it to be good. To the rescue comes a new and powerful tool: graphics presentation programs. These programs are designed to help you create an effective presentation, whether to the board of directors of your company or to your fellow classmates. An effective presentation gets your point across clearly and in an interesting manner.

The use of graphics presentation software has been increasing dramatically in the past few years. Three of the most popular graphics presentation programs today are Lotus' Freelance Graphics, Corel Presentations, and Microsoft's PowerPoint.

Definition of Graphics Presentation Programs

Graphics presentation programs are designed to help you produce a high-quality presentation that is both interesting to the audience and effective in its ability to convey your message. A presentation can be as simple as overhead transparencies or as sophisticated as an on-screen electronic display. Graphics presentation programs can produce black-and-white or color overhead transparencies, 35mm slides, on-screen electronic presentations called screen shows, and support materials for both the speaker and the audience.

The graphics presentation program includes features such as text handling, outlining, graphing, drawing, animations, clip art and multimedia support. With a few keystrokes the user can quickly change, correct, and update the presentation. In addition, graphics presentation programs suggest layouts for different types of presentations and offer professionally designed templates to help you produce a presentation that is sure to keep your audience's attention.

Features of Graphics Presentation Programs

Creating an effective presentation is a complicated process. Graphics presentation programs help simplify this process by providing assistance in the content development phase, as well as the layout and design phase. In addition, these programs produce the support materials you can use when making a presentation to an audience.

The content development phase includes deciding on the topic of your presentation, the organization of the content, and the ultimate message you want to convey to the audience. As an aid in this phase, some graphics presentation programs help you organize your thoughts based on the type of presentation you are making. Several common types of presentations sell a product or idea, suggest a strategy, or report on the progress of a program. Based on the type of presentation, the program suggests ideas and organization tips. For example, if you are making a presentation on the progress of a sales campaign, the program would suggest that you enter text on the background of the sales campaign as the first page, called a slide; the current status of the campaign as the next slide; and accomplishments, schedule, issues and problems, and where you are heading on subsequent slides.

The layout for each slide is the next important decision. Some graphics presentation programs help you by suggesting text layout features such as title placement, bullets, and columns. You can also incorporate graphs of data, tables, organizational charts, clip art, and other special text effects in the slides.

Most programs also include professionally designed templates to further enhance the appearance of your slides. These templates include features that standardize the appearance of all the slides in your presentation. Professionally selected combinations of text and background colors, common typefaces and sizes, borders, and other art designs take the worry out of much of the design layout.

Once you have written and designed the slides, you can then have the slides made into black-and-white or color overhead transparencies or 35mm slides. Alternatively, you can use the slides in an on-screen electronic presentation. An electronic presentation uses the computer to display the slides on an overhead projection screen. When using this type of presentation, many programs also include a rehearsal feature. This feature lets you practice and time your presentation. The length of time to display each slide can be set and your entire presentation can be completed within the allotted time.

Finally, these programs also allow you to produce printouts of the materials you have created. You can print an outline of the text showing the titles of the slides and main text but not the art. The outline allows you to check the organizational logic of your presentation. You can also print speaker notes that you can refer to while making your presentation. These notes generally consist of a small printout of each slide with any notes on topics you want to discuss while the slides are displayed. Finally, you can create printed handouts of the slides for the audience. The audience can refer to the slide and make notes on the page as you speak.

Graphics Presentation Terminology

The following terms are generic in nature and are associated with most graphic presentation programs.

Handout: Small printed version of slides for audience use during the presentation.

Layout: The styles, such as colors and fonts, applied to a slide that control how entries in the slide are displayed.

Outline: Displays the titles and text in each slide without the art.

Presentation: A collection of slides, handouts, notes, and outline, all in one file.

Rehearsal feature: Allows you to practice and time your presentation.

Screen show: An on-screen electronic presentation.

Slide: Individual "page" of the presentation, which can include text, art, graphs, and so on.

Speaker notes: Small printed version of each slide plus any notes the speaker has entered to refer to while making the presentation.

Case Study for Labs 1–3

As a recent college graduate, you have accepted your first job as a management trainee for The Sports Company. The Sports Company is a chain of discount sporting goods stores located in large metropolitan areas throughout the United States. The management trainee program emphasis is on computer applications in the area of retail management and requires that you work in several areas of the company.

In this series of labs, you are working in the marketing department. You have recently completed a project analyzing past, present, and future sales. The marketing manager has asked you to prepare a presentation for the weekly sales meeting about your findings. The company has recently purchased the graphics presentation program Microsoft PowerPoint 97. You will use this package to create the presentation.

In Lab 1 you use PowerPoint to enter and edit the text for your presentation. You also learn how to delete and move slides and to run a slide show.

In Lab 2 you enhance the appearance of your slides by adding clip art and graphs. You also learn how to add transitional effects to make the presentation more interesting. Finally, you create speaker notes to help you keep your cool during the presentation.

Lab 3 demonstrates the sharing of information between applications. First you learn how to link a chart created in Excel to a PowerPoint slide. Then you learn how to embed a PowerPoint slide presentation in a Word document.

Before You Begin

To the Student

The following assumptions have been made:

- The Microsoft PowerPoint 97 program has been properly installed on the hard disk of your computer system. A mouse is also installed.

- Your student data disk contains the files needed to complete the series of labs. These files are supplied by your instructor.

- You have completed the McGraw-Hill Windows 95 lab module or you are already familiar with how to use Windows 95 and a mouse.

To the Instructor

Please be aware that the following settings are assumed to be in effect for PowerPoint 97. These assumptions are necessary so that the screens and directions in the manual are accurate.

- Microsoft PowerPoint 97 has been installed using the default program settings.

- The Screen Tips feature is active (Use Tools/Options/View).

- The Clip Art gallery is installed.

- The Office Assistant is on.

- The Common Tasks toolbar is not on.

- The Additional Content templates have been installed.

- In addition, all figures in the manual reflect the use of a standard VGA display setting (640 x 480) and an Epson AP5000 printer. If another monitor type is used, there may be more lines of text displayed in the windows than in the figures. This setting can be changed using Windows setup. The selected printer also affects how text appears onscreen. If possible, select a printer and monitor type that will match the figures in the manual.

Microsoft Office Shortcut Bar

The Microsoft Office Shortcut Bar (shown below) may be displayed automatically on the Windows desktop. Commonly, it appears in the upper right section of the desktop; however, it may appear in other locations, depending upon your setup. Because the Shortcut Bar can be customized, it may display different buttons than shown below.

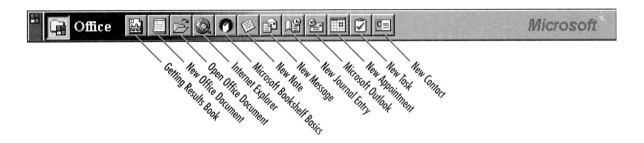

The Office Shortcut Bar makes it easy to open existing documents or to create new documents using one of the Microsoft Office applications. It can also be used to send e-mail, add a task to a to-do list, schedule appointments using Outlook, or add contacts or notes.

Instructional Conventions

This text uses the following instructional conventions:

■ Steps that you are to perform are preceded with a bullet (■) and are in blue type.

■ Command sequences you are to issue appear following the word "Choose." Each menu command selection is separated by a /. If the command can be selected by typing a letter of the command, the letter will appear bold and underlined.

■ Commands that can be initiated using a button and the mouse appear following the word "Click." The menu equivalent and keyboard shortcut appear in a margin note when the action is first introduced.

■ Anything you are to type appears in bold text.

Creating a Presentation

CASE STUDY

As a recent college graduate, you have accepted your first job as a management trainee for The Sports Company, a chain of discount sporting goods stores located in large metropolitan areas throughout the United States. Your present position is in the marketing department of The Sports Company. You have recently completed a project that analyzed the past, present, and future sales for the firm.

The marketing department manager has just informed you that you will present your findings tomorrow at the weekly sales meeting. To help you create the presentation, you will use PowerPoint 97, a graphics presentation application that is designed to create high-quality and interesting presentation materials that will dazzle your audience. Several screens of your presentation are shown here.

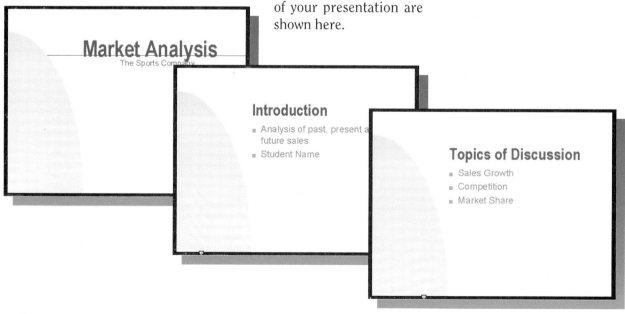

Concept Overview

The following concepts will be introduced in this lab:

1. Presentation Development   The development of a presentation follows several steps: plan, create, edit, enhance, and rehearse.

2. Types of Presentations   You can use PowerPoint to create on-screen presentations, black-and-white or color overhead transparencies, and 35mm slides.

3. Slides   A slide is an individual "page" of your presentation. The first slide of a presentation is the title slide. Additional slides are used to support each main point in your presentation.

4. Presentation Views   PowerPoint provides five different views that are used to look at and modify your presentation.

5. Spelling Checker   PowerPoint automatically checks the spelling of each word as you type by checking the word against the main and custom dictionaries.

6. Fonts   A font is a set of characters with a specific design. Using fonts as a design element can add interest to your presentation.

Part 1

Loading PowerPoint

The Sports Company has just purchased the graphics presentation program, Microsoft PowerPoint 97. Using this program you should have no problem creating a presentation for tomorrow's meeting.

■ If necessary, turn on your computer and put your data disk in drive A (or the appropriate drive for your system).

■ Click Start.

■ Choose Programs/ Microsoft PowerPoint .

 If a Shortcut to Microsoft PowerPoint PowerPoint button is displayed on your desktop, you can double-click the button to start the program.

After a few moments, the PowerPoint application window with the startup dialog box open in it as shown in Figure 1-1 is displayed.

FIGURE 1-1

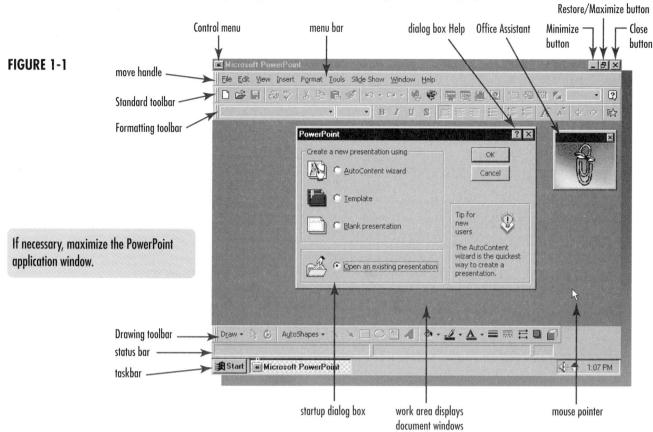

If necessary, maximize the PowerPoint application window.

The PowerPoint application window has many of the same features as in Windows 95 and other Microsoft products. Among those features are a title bar, menu bar, toolbars, document window, Minimize ▢, Restore/Maximize ▣, and Close ☒ buttons, and mouse capability. You can move and size PowerPoint windows, select commands, and use Help, just as in other Windows 95 applications. The taskbar at the bottom of your screen allows you to switch between other open applications and to access the Windows 95 desktop. Your knowledge of Windows 95 makes learning and using PowerPoint much easier.

The initial PowerPoint window that is displayed is called the main window. The menu bar below the title bar displays the PowerPoint program menu, which consists of nine menus. The left end of the menu bar displays the document window Control-menu icon ▣, and the right end displays the document window Minimize ▢, Restore ▣, and Close ☒ buttons.

The window also includes three toolbars. As in other Office 97 applications, the Standard and Formatting toolbars appear below the menu bar. The **Standard toolbar** contains buttons that are shortcuts for many of the most frequently used menu commands. The **Formatting toolbar** contains buttons that are used to change the format or design of the text in the presentation. The **Drawing toolbar** is displayed along the bottom edge of the window. It contains buttons that are used to enhance text and create shapes. Most toolbars appear automatically as you perform different tasks and open different windows.

The left end of both the menu and the toolbars displays a **move handle** ⫼ that when dragged moves the menu or toolbar to another location. Both menu and toolbars can be **docked** (as they are now) or **floating**. When docked they are fixed to an edge of the window and display the move handle. When floating they appear in a separate window that can be moved by dragging the title bar.

The large area containing the startup dialog box is the **work area**. It is where your presentations are displayed as you create and edit them. The status bar at the bottom of the PowerPoint window displays messages and information about various PowerPoint settings. Currently the status bar is empty.

In addition, your screen may display the Office Assistant. This feature is discussed next.

Using the Office Assistant

As in all Microsoft applications, there are several ways to get onscreen help. For brief information about different screen elements, you can display a Screen Tip. Pointing to a toolbar button displays the button name in a Screen Tip box. For information on other window elements, you can use the What's This option on the Help menu and click on an element to display a brief description. To see a Screen Tip for a dialog box option, click the ? button in the title bar and then click the option. For example, using this feature in the Startup dialog box displays the Screen Tip about the AutoContent Wizard at the right.

toolbar —— Screen Tip

dialog box —— Screen Tip

Another method of getting Help in all Office 97 programs is through the **Office Assistant**. The Office Assistant is used to get help on features that are specific to the Office application you are using. The Assistant can display tips that point out how to use the features or keyboard shortcuts more effectively. A tip is available when a yellow light bulb 💡 appears in the Assistant; click the light bulb to see the tip. It can also automatically display help suggestions based on your actions. In addition, you can activate the Assistant at any time to ask for help on any topic. To activate it,

■ Click  Office Assistant.

A yellow balloon displays a prompt and a text box in which you can type the topic on which you want help. In addition, the Tips option button displays the most recent tip and lets you scroll through tips that the Office Assistant has recently displayed. The Options button is used to change Office Assistant so it provides different levels of help.

PRESENTATION

Your tip may be different than displayed here.

- Click (Tips) and read the tip that appears in the box.

- To clear the tip, click (Close).

Next you will use the Assistant to find out what types of items you can create using PowerPoint.

- Click Office Assistant.

- Type **What does PowerPoint make**

- Click (Search).

- Select What you can create with PowerPoint.

Your screen should be similar to Figure 1-2.

FIGURE 1-2

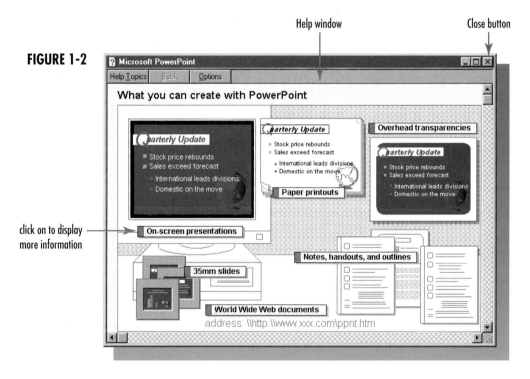

click on to display more information

The Office Assistant displays a Help window with several topic boxes that you can click on to get more information.

The mouse pointer changes to a 🖑 when pointing to a box.

- Click on each box to learn about the different items that can be created using PowerPoint.

- When you are done, close the Help window.

You can leave the Office Assistant open or you can close it and activate it when needed. This text will not display the Assistant open.

- If you want to hide the Assistant, click ☒ in the Assistant's window.

Planning a Presentation

During your presentation you will present findings from a project you recently completed. This project analyzed the company's past, present, and future sales. As you prepare to create a new presentation, you should follow several basic steps.

Concept 1: Presentation Development

The development of a presentation follows several steps: plan, create, edit, enhance, and rehearse.

Plan: The first step in planning a presentation is to understand its purpose. You also need to find out the length of time you have to speak, who the audience is, what type of room you will be in, and what kind of audiovisual equipment is available. These factors have an impact on the type of presentation you will create.

Create: To begin creating your presentation, develop the content by typing your thoughts or notes into an outline. Each main idea in your presentation should have a supporting slide with a title and bulleted points.

Edit: While typing you are bound to make typing and spelling errors that need to be corrected. This is one type of editing. Another is to revise the content of what you have entered to make it clearer, or to add or delete information. To do this you might insert a slide, add or delete bulleted items, or move text to another location.

Enhance: You want to develop a presentation that grabs and holds the audience's attention. Choose a design that gives your presentation some dazzle. Wherever possible add graphics to replace or enhance text. Add slide transitions, which control how a slide appears and disappears, and build slides, which reveal text in a bulleted list one bullet at a time.

Rehearse: Finally, you should rehearse the delivery of your presentation. For a professional presentation, your delivery should be as polished as your materials. Use the same equipment that you will use when you give the presentation. Practice advancing from slide to slide and then back in case someone asks a question. If you have a mouse available, practice pointing or drawing on the slide to call attention to key points.

After rehearsing your presentation, you may find that you want to go back to the editing phase. You may change text, move bullets, or insert a new slide. Each time you make a change, rehearse the entire presentation again. By the day of the presentation, you will be confident about your message and at ease with the materials.

The purpose of your presentation is to summarize the company's sales activity. In addition, you want to impress the marketing department manager by creating a professional presentation.

PRESENTATION

Using the AutoContent Wizard

The startup dialog box is used to specify how you want to start using the PowerPoint program. It includes three options that provide access to different methods you can use to create a new presentation. The preselected option, AutoContent Wizard, is a guided approach that helps you determine the content and organization of your presentation through a series of questions. Then it creates a presentation that contains suggested content and design based on the answers you provide.

You can also create a new presentation beginning with a design template, which is a file containing predefined settings that determine the presentation's color scheme, fonts, and other design features. Finally, you can create a new presentation beginning with a blank presentation, with the color scheme, fonts, and other design features set to default values. As suggested in the startup dialog box tip, you will use the AutoContent Wizard.

> You will learn more about design templates in Lab 2.

> If the Microsoft Office Suite is on your system and the Office Shortcut Bar is displayed, you can click 🖉 Start a New Document and select the method you want to use to create a new presentation while loading the PowerPoint program.

■ Select **A**utoContent Wizard.

■ Click ◖ OK ◗.

The first AutoContent Wizard dialog box on your screen should be similar to Figure 1-3.

FIGURE 1-3

green indicates —— current steps

outline of steps —— to create a presentation

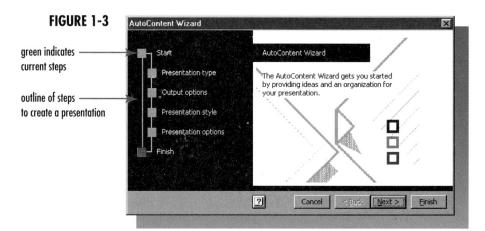

> The menu equivalent is **F**ile/**N**ew/ Presentation/AutoContent Wizard.

> You can also click the outline box on the left side to move directly to any step.

As the AutoContent Wizard guides you through creating the presentation, it shows you which step you are on in the outline on the left side of the window. The green box identifies the current step. To move on to the next step,

■ Choose ◖ Next > ◗.

Your screen should be similar to Figure 1-4.

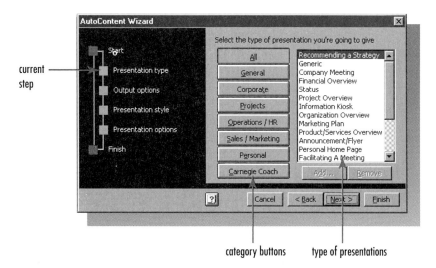

current step

category buttons   type of presentations

FIGURE 1-4

In the second AutoContent Wizard dialog box, you are asked to select the type of presentation you are creating. You can select one of 20 different types of presentations. Each type has a different recommended content and design. Currently, all the presentation types are listed. Each type is also indexed under a category.

■   Click on each category button to see how the presentation types are organized.

The presentation you are creating is a report of the firm's market analysis. You will use the Generic presentation option.

■   Click [All] .

■   Select Generic.

■   Click [Next >] .

From the third AutoContent Wizard dialog box, you can select how the presentation will be made; in person in a meeting, or online (such as on the Internet) to be viewed without your being present. Your presentation will be presented in person.

■   If necessary, select Presentations, informal meetings, handouts.

■   Click [Next >] .

The Generic option is also available under the General category.

The fourth AutoContent Wizard dialog box on your screen should be similar to Figure 1-5.

FIGURE 1-5

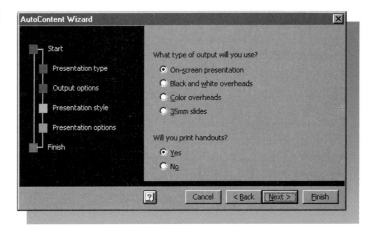

In this dialog box, you select the type of output your presentation will use.

Concept 2: Types of Presentations

You can use PowerPoint to create on-screen presentations, black-and-white or color overhead transparencies, and 35mm slides. The type of equipment that is available to you will have an impact on the type of presentation you create.

If you have computer projection equipment, which displays the current monitor image on a screen, you should create a full-color on-screen presentation. Often you will have access only to an overhead projector, in which case you can create color or black-and-white overhead transparencies. Most laser printers will print your overheads directly on plastic transparencies, or you can print your slides and have transparencies made at a copy center. If you have access to a slide projector, you may want to use 35mm slides. You can send your presentation to a service bureau that will create the slides for you.

Because the room you will be using to make your presentation is equipped with computer projection equipment, you will create an on-screen presentation. The Wizard selects the color scheme best suited to the type of output you select. In addition, you also plan to provide handouts. **Handouts** are small printed copies of each page of your presentation that can be used by the audience while listening to your presentation. Since these are the default selections, to accept them and move to the next step,

■   Click .

Your screen should be similar to Figure 1-6.

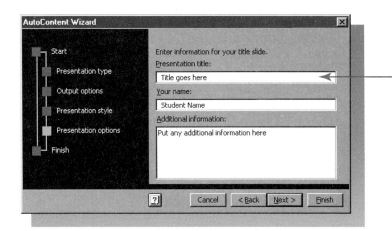

enter presentation
in title text box

The default information in the dialog box displayed on your screen may be different from the information displayed in Figure 1-6.

In the fifth AutoContent Wizard dialog box, you are asked to enter some basic information that will appear on the first slide of the presentation.

Concept 3: Slides

A **slide** is an individual "page" of your presentation. The first slide of a presentation is the title slide. It is used to introduce your presentation. Additional slides are used to support each main point in your presentation. The slides give the audience a visual summary of the words you speak, which helps them understand the content and keeps them entertained. The slides also help you, the speaker, organize your thoughts, and prompt you during the presentation.

- Replace the default information in the Presentation title text box with **Market Analysis**.

- Enter your name as the author.

- Enter **The Sports Company** in the Additional Information text box.

- Click   Next > .

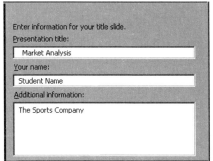

Click on the text box to move to it, and select the text by dragging. Use Tab to move to the next text box and also automatically select the entry.

If you make a typing error, use the Backspace key to delete the characters to the left of the insertion point and then retype the correct text.

You have entered all the information PowerPoint needs to create your presentation.

- Click   Finish .

Viewing the Presentation

Based on your selections and entries, the AutoContent Wizard creates a presentation and displays it in a document window in the work area.
Your screen should be similar to Figure 1-7.

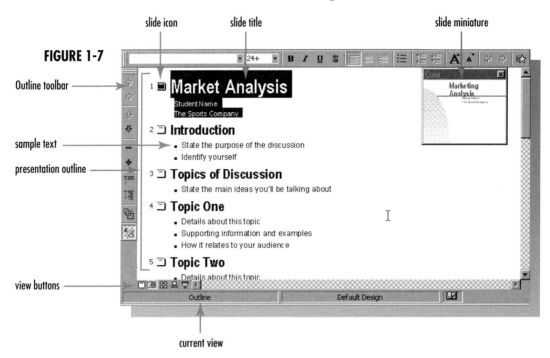

FIGURE 1-7

- slide icon
- slide title
- slide miniature
- Outline toolbar
- sample text
- presentation outline
- view buttons
- current view

■   If necessary, maximize the document window.

> The status bar displays the name of the current view.

The presentation is displayed in Outline view. This is one of five views available in PowerPoint.

Concept 4: Presentation Views

PowerPoint provides five different **views** you can use to look at and modify your presentation. Depending on what you are doing, one view may be preferable to another. The commands to change views are located in the View menu. In addition, to the left of the horizontal scroll bar are five view buttons that are used to quickly switch from one view to another. The buttons and views are described below.

Button	View	Description
▣	Slide	Each presentation slide is shown in its final form. This view is typically used to enter and edit the content and appearance of the presentation.
▤	Outline	Presents the content of the presentation in a standard outline format. It is typically used to enter and edit the presentation's content. A miniature of the slide is also displayed.
▦	Slide Sorter	A miniature of each slide is presented. It is typically used to reorder slides, add special effects such as transitions, and set timing between slides.
▣	Note Pages	Like Slide view, each slide is shown in its final form. The size of the slide is much smaller, however, and space is available to insert speaker notes.
▣	Slide Show	Used to practice or to present the presentation. It displays each slide in final form.

Outline view displays in outline format the title and text for each slide in the presentation. This view is used to organize and develop the content for your presentation. In Outline view the Drawing toolbar has been replaced with the **Outline toolbar**. This toolbar contains buttons (identified on the right) that make it easier to modify the outline.

To the left of each slide title is a slide icon ▭ and number that identifies each slide (see Figure 1-7). The text for the first slide, consisting of the title and text you specified when using the AutoContent Wizard, is selected. A miniature of this slide is also displayed.

The other slides in the outline contain sample text that was included by the Wizard based upon the type of presentation you selected. The sample text suggests the content for each slide to help you organize your presentation's con-

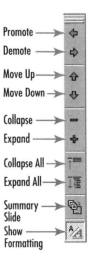

tent. For example, the second slide recommends an opening statement to explain the purpose of the discussion and to introduce yourself.

■ Click "Introduction."

The slide miniature now displays the second slide.

Editing a Presentation in Outline View

You need to replace the sample text with the appropriate information for your presentation. In addition to the usual methods of selecting text, such as dragging, in Outline view you can quickly select an entire paragraph and all subparagraphs by triple clicking on a line or by pointing to the left of the line and clicking when the mouse pointer is a ⁺↕⁺. In addition, you can click the slide icon ▭ to the right of the slide number to select all text on the slide.

■ Using one of these methods, select the sample text, "State the purpose of the discussion."

To enter the purpose for your presentation (this word is intentionally misspelled),

■ Type **Analsis**

Your screen should be similar to Figure 1-8.

> In Outline view the mouse pointer appears as ▹ an arrow, I an I-beam, or ⁺↕⁺ a four-arrow pointer.

> The selection and editing procedures used in PowerPoint are the same as in Word or most other word processors.

> If you accidentally drag selected text, it will move. To return it to its original location, use the Undo command on the Edit menu or the ⟲ Undo toolbar button.

> As you make changes to the outline, the slide miniature updates immediately.

text updated in slide miniature

misspelled word identified by wavy underline

Arial | **28** | **B** *I* <u>U</u> **S**

1 ▭ **Market Analysis**
    Student Name
    The Sports Company

2 ▭ **Introduction**
    ▪ Analsis
    ▪ Identify yourself

3 ▭ **Topics of Discussion**
    ▪ State the main ideas you'll be talking about

4 ▭ **Topic One**
    ▪ Details about this topic
    ▪ Supporting information and examples
    ▪ How it relates to your audience

5 ▭ **Topic Two**
    ▪ Details about this topic.

Outline | Default Design

indicates a spelling error has been found

FIGURE 1-8

As you enter text, the program checks the word for accuracy. PowerPoint has identified the word as a misspelled word by underlining it with a wavy red line. In addition, the spelling indicator in the status bar appears as ▨, indicating a spelling error has been found.

The ▨ indicator means no spelling errors have been found.

Concept 5: Spelling Checker

PowerPoint includes a Spelling Checker tool that automatically checks the spelling of each word as you type against words in a **main dictionary** that is included with the PowerPoint program. If the word does not appear in the main dictionary, the program checks a **custom dictionary**, which you can create to hold words you commonly use but that are not included in the main dictionary.

If the word does not appear in either dictionary, the program identifies it as misspelled by displaying a wavy red line below the word. You can then correct the misspelled word by editing it. Alternatively, you can display a list of suggested spelling corrections for that word and select the correct spelling from the list to replace the misspelled word in the document.

The Spelling Checker works just as in the other Microsoft Office applications.

Because you have discovered this error very soon after typing it, and you know that the correct spelling of this word is "analysis," you can quickly correct it using Backspace. The Backspace key removes the character or space to the left of the insertion point; therefore, it is particularly useful when you are moving from right to left (backward) along a line of text. To correct this word, and continue entering the text for this slide,

- Press Backspace 3 times.

- Type **ysis**

- Press Spacebar.

- Type **of past, prsent**

As you type, an animated pen appears over the spelling indicator while the Spelling Checker is in the process of checking for errors.

Again, the program has identified a word as misspelled. Another way to quickly correct a misspelled word is to select the correct spelling from a list of suggested spelling corrections displayed on the Spelling Shortcut menu.

- Right-click on the word to display the Spelling shortcut menu.

This menu displays two suggested correct spellings. The menu also includes several related menu options. Ignore All instructs PowerPoint to ignore the misspelling of this word throughout the rest of this session, and Add adds the word to the custom dictionary list. When a word is added to the custom dictionary, PowerPoint will always accept that spelling as correct. The last option, Spelling, starts the Spelling Checker tool to check the entire document. You will learn about this feature later in this lab.

Sometimes there are no suggested replacements because PowerPoint cannot locate any words in its dictionary that are similar in spelling or the suggestions are not correct. If this happens, you need to edit the word manually. To replace the word with the correct spelling and complete the outline entry,

■ Click "present."

■ Clear the highlight.

■ Type **, and future sales**

To enter your name on this slide,

■ Select "Identify yourself."

■ Type **[your name]**

Your screen should be similar to Figure 1-9.

miniature slide text updated

FIGURE 1-9

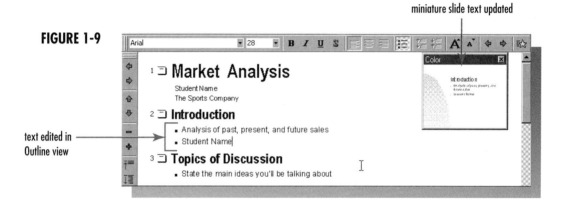

text edited in
Outline view

You realize that you now have your name on both the first and second slides of the presentation. You would like to remove your name from the first slide. To do this,

■ Select your name on slide 1.

■ Press Delete.

You are now ready to update the third slide in your presentation. You will be discussing three main topics: sales growth, competition, and market share. To enter these into the Topics of Discussion slide,

■ Select "State the main ideas you'll be talking about."

■ Type **Sales Growth**

■ Press ←Enter.

■ Type **Market Share**

■ Press ←Enter.

■ Type **Competition** (do not press ←Enter).

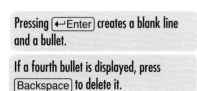

Pressing ←Enter creates a blank line and a bullet.

If a fourth bullet is displayed, press Backspace to delete it.

You realize that you entered the topics in the wrong order. You want to change the order of the second and third items in the list. A bulleted point can be moved easily by selecting it and dragging it to a new location or by using the ⬆ Move Up or ⬇ Move Down buttons in the Outline toolbar. To move the bulleted item on the current line up one line,

■   Click ⬆ Move up.

Your screen should be similar to Figure 1-10.

Move Up button

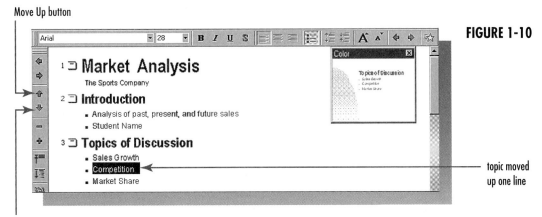

FIGURE 1-10

topic moved up one line

Move Down button

Although you can see the changes in the slide miniature, it is difficult to see because it is so small. To see an enlarged view of it, you will switch to Slide view.

■   Click 🔲 Slide View.

Your screen should be similar to Figure 1-11.

Pointing to a view button displays its name in a Screen Tip.

The menu equivalent is **V**iew/**S**lide.

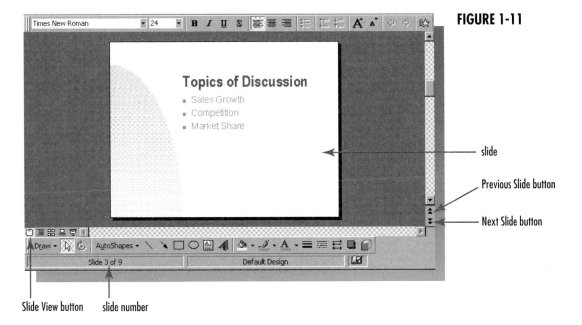

FIGURE 1-11

slide

Previous Slide button

Next Slide button

Slide View button   slide number

The slide you are on in Outline view is the slide that is displayed in Slide view.

The third slide is displayed in Slide view, and the status bar shows the current slide number and the total number of slides in the presentation. It is now much easier to see how the text appears in the slide as well as the slide design and colors. All the slides in the presentation use the same design style, associated with a generic presentation. The design style sets the background design and color, as well as the text style, color, and layout.

The following features can be used to move within Slide view:

Action	Result
Click ▲ or Click above scroll box or Press Page Up	Displays previous slide
Click ▼ or Click below scroll box or Press Page Down	Displays next slide
Drag scroll box	Displays slide indicated in slide indicator box

The ▲ Previous Slide and ▼ Next Slide buttons are located at the bottom of the vertical scroll bar.

Slide: 3 of 9
Topics of Discussion

■   Using any of the methods presented above, view the first two slides in Slide view.

Editing in Slide View

Now you want to continue to update the information in the presentation. You can also edit the slide content in Slide view.

■   Display slide 4.

The fourth slide contains the title "Topic One" and a list of three bulleted items. The title and the bulleted list are two separate elements or **placeholders** on the slide. Placeholders are boxes that are designed to contain specific types of items or **objects** such as the slide title, bulleted text, charts, tables, and pictures. Each slide can have several different types of placeholders. To indicate which place-holder to work with, you must first select it. You want to change the sample text in the title placeholder.

■   Click anywhere on the sample title text.

Your screen should be similar to Figure 1-12.

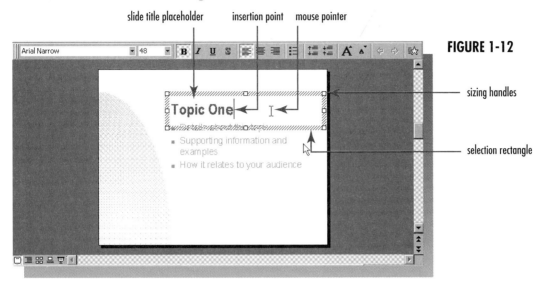

slide title placeholder   insertion point   mouse pointer

FIGURE 1-12

sizing handles

selection rectangle

The title placeholder is surrounded with **sizing handles** (eight boxes) and a **selection rectangle**. Dragging on the sizing handles changes the size of the placeholder. Because the title placeholder contains text, an insertion point also appears to show your location in the text and to allow you to select and edit the text. The mouse pointer appears as an I-beam to be used to position the insertion point. To enter the new title for this slide,

- Select the title text.

- Type **Sales Growth**

Next you need to replace the sample text in the bulleted list placeholder with the sales data.

- Click on any of the bulleted items.

- Select all three items in the placeholder.

- Type **1995 sales $5,100,000**

- Press ⏎Enter.

- Type **1996 sales $5,900,000**

- Press ⏎Enter.

- Type **1997 sales $7,400,000**

- Press ⏎Enter.

- Type **1998 sales $10,200,000** (do not press ⏎Enter).

To deselect a placeholder, click anywhere outside the selected placeholder.

Drag to select a portion of the text or triple-click to select a line.

Drag to select multiple lines of text.

If you accidentally press ⏎Enter and a fifth bullet is displayed, press Backspace to delete it.

PRESENTATION

Your screen should be similar to Figure 1-13.

FIGURE 1-13

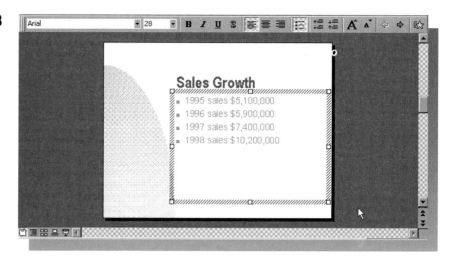

■ Display the fifth slide.

You want this slide to display the names of the companies that are competitors of The Sports Company, the year they opened, and their home office location.

■ In place of the sample title text, type **Competition**

■ Click on any bulleted item.

You can select the bulleted items by dragging the mouse over them as you did in the previous slide, or you can use the Edit/Select All command shortcut key, Ctrl + A. To do this,

> The menu equivalent is **Edit/Select All.**

■ Press Ctrl + A.

All three bulleted items inside the selected placeholder are selected. To enter the replacement text for the first bulleted item,

■ Type **Action Corporation**

■ Press ←Enter.

You want the next bulleted item to be indented below the first bulleted item. Indenting a bulleted item to the right **demotes** it, or makes it a lower or subordinate topic in the outline hierarchy.

> The ➡ Demote button is on the Formatting toolbar.

■ Click ➡ Demote (Indent more).

demoted item appears as indented bullet

The bullet style of the demoted line has changed to a ◆. To enter the next two lines of text,

> When you demote a bulleted item, PowerPoint continues to indent to the same level until you cancel the indent.

■ Type **established in 1986**

■ Press ←Enter.

- Type **located in Union, Oregon**
- Press [←Enter].

You are ready to enter the information for the second competitor. Before entering the company name, you want to remove the indentation, or **promote** the line. Promoting a line moves it to the left, or up a level in the outline hierarchy.

- Click ⬅ Promote (Indent less).
- Type **Teams Unlimited**
- Press [←Enter].
- Type **established in 1989**
- Click ➡ Demote (Indent more).
- Press [←Enter].
- Type **located in Spring, Maine**
- To clear the selection, click outside the selection.

Your screen should be similar to Figure 1-14.

You can also demote and promote bulleted items in Outline view using the ➡ and ⬅ buttons.

The insertion point can be anywhere on the line to be promoted or demoted.

You can also press [Tab ↹] or [⇧Shift] + [Tab ↹] to demote or promote it.

Demote button

Promote button

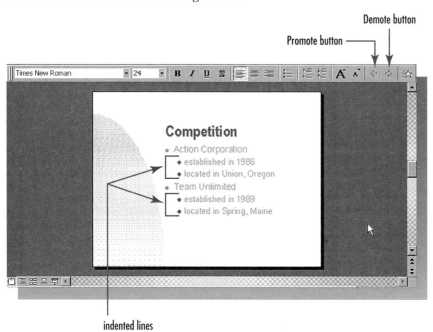

FIGURE 1-14

indented lines

Saving a Presentation

You have just been notified of an important meeting that is to begin in just a few minutes. Before leaving for the meeting you want to save the presentation as a file on your data disk. You can use the Save or Save As command on the File menu. The Save command or the 🖫 Save button will save the current document to disk using the same file name. The Save As command allows you to save the current document to disk using a new file name. Because the presentation has not been saved yet, you can use either command.

The menu equivalent is **File**/**Save**, and the keyboard shortcut is Ctrl + S.

■   Click 🖫 Save.

The File Save dialog box on your screen should be similar to Figure 1-15.

default location to save file

FIGURE 1-15

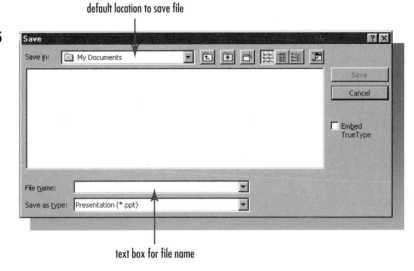

text box for file name

As in all Office applications, this dialog box is used to specify the location to save the file and the file name. You need to change the location to the drive containing your data disk.

■   Open the Save In drop-down list box.

■   Select drive A (or the appropriate drive for your system).

A PowerPoint file name follows the Windows 95 file naming rules. It is automatically saved with the file extension .ppt, which identifies it as a PowerPoint file.

Next you need to specify a name for the presentation document. In the File Name text box,

■   Type **Market Analysis Presentation**

■   Click [Save].

The new file name is displayed in the window title bar. The presentation that was on your screen and in the computer's memory is now saved on your data disk in a new file called Market Analysis Presentation. To close the saved presentation,

You can also click ☒ to close the window.

■   Choose **File**/**Close**.

The presentation is closed, and a blank PowerPoint window is displayed. Always save your slide presentation before closing a file or leaving the PowerPoint program. As a safeguard against losing your work if you forget to save the presentation, PowerPoint will remind you to save any unsaved presentation before closing the file or exiting the program.

Note: If you are ending your lab session now, choose **File**/**Exit** to exit the program. When you begin again, load PowerPoint and close the startup dialog box.

Part 2

Opening a Presentation

After returning from your meeting, you hastily continued to enter the information for several more slides. To see the information in the new slides,

■ Click 📂 Open.

In the Open dialog box you specify the name and location of the file you want to open.

■ If necessary, select the drive containing your data disk from the Look In drop-down list box.

The file names and folders displayed in the File Name list box are those on your data disk in the selected drive. The file you want to open is Marketing Presentation 1.

■ Select Marketing Presentation 1.

■ Click 〔　Open　〕.

Note: If the file name Marketing Presentation 1 is not displayed in the Name list box, ask your instructor for help.

Using the Spelling Checker

■ Edit slide 2 to display your name.

As you entered the information in the additional slides, you left several typing errors uncorrected. The automatic Spelling Checker feature will identify those errors as you move to the slide. However, you can also activate the Spelling Checker at any time by clicking 🔤 or using the Spelling command on the Tools menu. Another method is to click on the spelling indicator 🔲 in the status bar. Using this method moves to the first potential spelling error and displays the spelling shortcut menu.

■ Double-click .

The menu equivalent is **F**ile/**O**pen and the keyboard shortcut is 〔Ctrl〕 + O. You can also select "Open an existing presentation" from the Startup dialog box when PowerPoint is first loaded.

If necessary, scroll the Name list box until the file name is displayed.

The Spelling Checker identifies many proper names as misspelled. To stop this from occurring, add those names to your custom dictionary.

The keyboard shortcut is 〔F7〕.

Your screen should be similar to Figure 1-16.

FIGURE 1-16

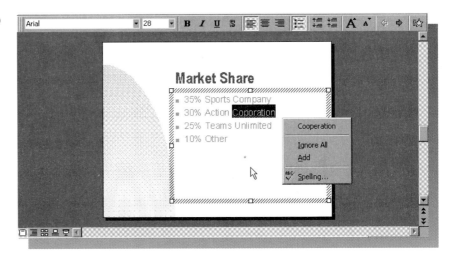

The program jumps to slide 6, which shows the market share percentage of The Sports Company and its competitors. The misspelled word "Coporation" is identified, and the Spelling Shortcut menu is open. However, the suggested replacement is not the correct word. You will use the Spelling dialog box to correct the spelling error.

■   Choose **S**pelling.

The Spelling dialog box on your screen should be similar to Figure 1-17.

FIGURE 1-17

misspelled word

suggested word

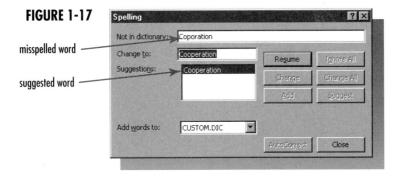

The misspelled word "Coporation" is identified in the dialog box as not being in the dictionary and the Suggestions box lists the possible replacement. Since the suggested replacement is incorrect, you need to correct this misspelling manually.

■   Type **Corporation** in the Change To text box.

To proceed, you need to choose one of the option buttons described below.

Option	Action
Ignore	Accepts the highlighted word in the document as correct for this occurrence only.
Ignore All	Accepts the highlighted word in the document as correct throughout the spell-check of this document.
Change	Enters the word displayed in the Change To text box in place of the highlighted word in the document.
Change All	Enters the word displayed in the Change To text box in place of the highlighted word throughout the spell-check of this document.
Add	Adds the word to the custom dictionary. When a word is added to the custom dictionary, the Spelling tool will always accept the added word as correct.
Suggest	Suggests replacement words if the Suggestions check box is turned off.

■ Click | Change |.

Once the Spelling dialog box is open, the Spelling Checker tool continues to check the entire document for spelling errors. The next misspelled word, "Stremgths," is identified. In this case the suggested replacement is correct.

> If necessary, move the dialog box to see the located misspelled word.

■ Click | Change |.

The next misspelled word is identified, and "Weaknesses" is the correct replacement.

■ Click | Change |.

There should be no other misspelled words. However, if the spelling tool encounters others in your file, correct them as needed. When no others are located, PowerPoint will display a message box telling you that spell-check has finished. To close the message box,

■ Click | OK |.

Deleting Slides

To get a better overall view of the slides in the presentation, you can switch to Slide Sorter view.

■ Click ⊞ Slide Sorter View.

> The menu equivalent is **V**iew/Sli**d**e Sorter.

Your screen should be similar to Figure 1-18.

FIGURE 1-18

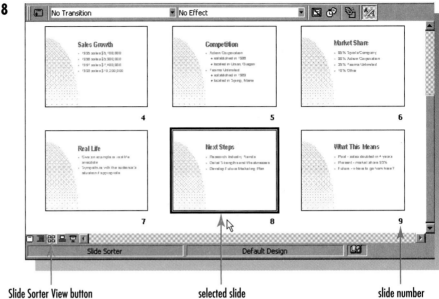

Slide Sorter View button   selected slide   slide number

Additional slides can be viewed by scrolling the window.

This view also has its own toolbar that is used to add enhancements to your presentation. You will learn about these features in Lab 2.

Clicking on a slide selects it.

The menu equivalent is **E**dit/**D**elete Slide.

You can also delete slides in Slide view using the same procedure.

This view displays a miniature of each slide in the presentation in the window. Viewing the slides side by side helps you see how your presentation flows. Now you can see that you need to delete slide 7 since you do not have any real-life examples that you want to add to your presentation. The slide number appears below each slide. Notice slide 8, the slide you were last viewing in Slide view, is displayed with a dark border around it. This indicates that the slide is selected. To select slide 7 and delete it,

- Select slide 7.
- Press ⌈Delete⌋.

The Real Life slide has been deleted, and slides 8 and 9 have been appropriately renumbered. There are now eight slides in the presentation.

Moving Slides

Next you decide to switch the order of slide 8, What This Means, with slide 7, Next Steps. To reorder slides in Slide Sorter view, drag a slide to its new location using drag and drop. As you drag the mouse pointer, an indicator line appears to show you where the slide will appear in the presentation. When the indicator line is located where you want the slide to be placed, release the mouse button.

■   Select slide 7.

■   Drag the mouse pointer to after slide 8.

Your screen should be similar to Figure 1-19.

You can also use the Cut and Paste commands on the Edit menu to move slides in Slide Sorter view.

FIGURE 1-19

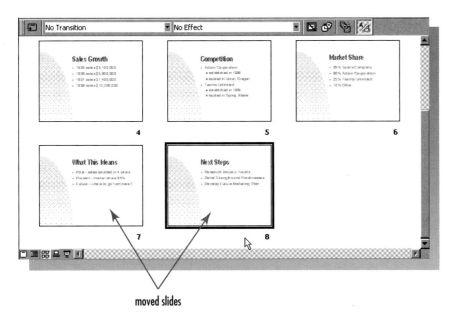

moved slides

Running a Slide Show

Now that the slides are in the order you want, you would like to display the presentation electronically as a slide show. A **slide show** is an on-screen display of your presentation. Each slide fills the screen, hiding the PowerPoint application window, so you can view the slides as your audience would. To begin the slide show starting with the first slide,

■   Select slide 1.

■   Click 🖳 Slide Show.

Use the scroll bar to scroll the Slide Sorter view window.

The menu equivalent is <u>V</u>iew/Slide Sho<u>w</u>.

Your screen should be similar to Figure 1-20.

FIGURE 1-20

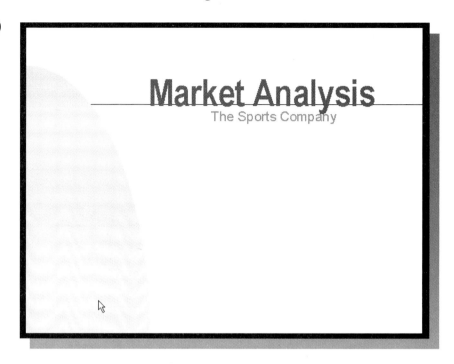

The presentation title slide is displayed full screen as it will appear when projected on a screen using computer projection equipment. The easiest way to see the next slide is to click the mouse button. You could also press Spacebar or Page Down or select Next from the Shortcut menu.

- ■ Click to display the next slide.
- ■ Using each of the methods described, slowly display the rest of the presentation.

After the last slide is displayed, the program returns to the view you were last using, in this case Slide Sorter view.

Adding a Slide Footer

You would also like the company name, date of the presentation, and slide numbers displayed on the bottom of each slide in a footer. A **footer** is text or graphics that appears at the bottom of each slide.

- ■ Choose **V**iew/**H**eader and Footer.
- ■ Open the Slide tab, if necessary.

The Header and Footer dialog box on your screen should be similar to Figure 1-21.

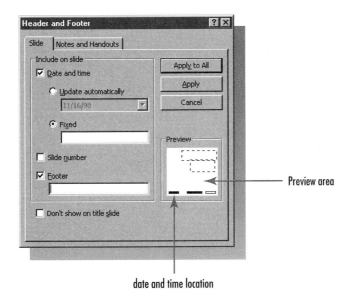

FIGURE 1-21

Preview area

date and time location

The Date and Time option is already selected. The two date and time options allow you to update the date automatically using the current system date and time or to enter a fixed date that will not change. Fixed is the selected default, but because the text box is empty, this information does not appear on your slides. To specify the date of the presentation, you will enter a permanent date.

If the Date and Time option and the Fixed option are not the default selections on your screen, select them.

■ Enter the current date in the Fixed text box.

You also want to include the slide number and the company name. To add this information to the footer,

■ Select Slide **N**umber.

■ Type **The Sports Company** in the Footer text box.

Notice that the Preview area of the dialog box displays three solid boxes where the footer information will appear on the slide. The date appears aligned with the left margin, the slide number at the right margin, and the footer text is centered. You do not, however, want this information displayed on the title slide.

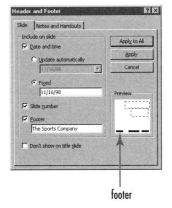

■ Select Don't show on title slide.

■ Click Apply to All .

The Apply command button applies the footer settings to the current slide only.

footer

Your screen should be similar to Figure 1-22.

FIGURE 1-22

no footer on
title slide

footers on all
other slides

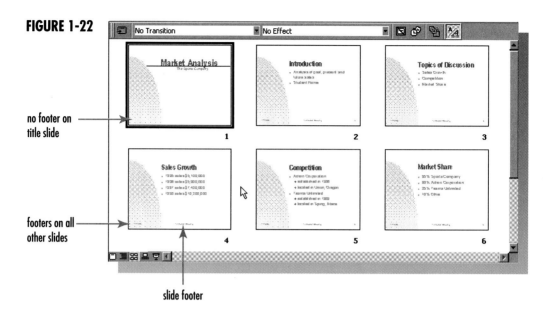

slide footer

To see make the footer easier to see,

■   Select slide 2.

■   Switch to Slide view.

Changing Font Size

■   Display slide 1.

While looking at the title slide, you decide its appearance could be improved by changing the font design and increasing the size of the subtitle text.

Concept 6: Fonts

A **font** is a set of characters with a specific design. The designs have names such as Times New Roman and Arial. Using fonts as a design element can add interest to your presentation. There are two basic types of fonts, serif and sans serif. **Serif fonts** have a flair at the base of each letter that visually leads the reader to the next letter. Serif fonts generally are for the main part of your presentation as they are easy to read. **Sans serif fonts** do not have a flair at the base of each letter. Because sans serif fonts have a clean look, they generally are used for headings to grab the audience's attention. Try not to use more than three different fonts in your presentation.

Each font has one or more sizes. **Font size** is the height of the character and is commonly measured in **points**, abbreviated "pt." One point equals about 1/72 inch, and text in most presentations starts at 24 points. For headings on your slides, you should use 48 to 60 points. Some common fonts in different sizes are shown below.

This is Arial 12 pt.

This is Arial 24 pt.

This is Arial 36 pt.

This is Times New Roman 12 pt.

This is Times New Roman 24 pt.

This is Times New Roman 36 pt.

To change the font for existing text, you must first select the text you want to change. You will change the font of the subtitle to Times New Roman with a size of 44 points.

- Select the subtitle text "The Sports Company."

- Open the `Arial` Font drop-down list.

- Choose Times New Roman.

- Open the `24` Font Size drop-down list.

- Choose 44.

To change font settings before typing the text, use the command and then type. All text will appear in the specified font and font size until another is selected.

The menu equivalent is F**o**rmat/**F**ont.

If the selection included text in several different sizes, the smallest size would appear followed by a + sign in the Font Size text box.

Your screen should be similar to Figure 1-23.

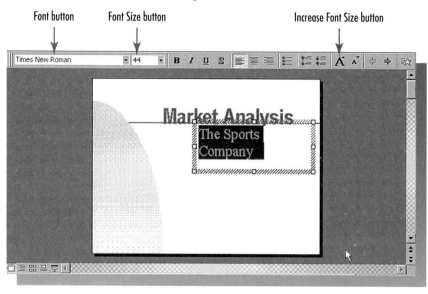

Font button   Font Size button   Increase Font Size button

FIGURE 1-23

The selected text is displayed in a different font and a larger type size. The Font button displays the selected font, and Font Size button displays the point size of the selection.

The [A] Increase Font Size button will incrementally increase the point size of selected text.

Sizing and Moving a Placeholder

Now, however, the subtitle text wraps to a second line in the placeholder because it is larger than the width of the placeholder. To fix this you will increase the placeholder size. You also want to move the subtitle down slightly to separate it more from the main title.

To adjust the placeholder size, drag the sizing handles. The corner handles will adjust both the height and width at the same time, whereas the center handles adjust the side borders to which they are associated. The placeholder needs to be longer only.

The mouse pointer appears as ←→, indicating the direction you can drag to adjust the size.

The mouse pointer appears as ⟪ when you can move a placeholder.

You can also move a selected placeholder by holding down (Ctrl) and pressing the directional keys.

■ Point to the left center handle and drag to the left.

When the placeholder is large enough, the subtitle will display on a single line. Next you want to move the placeholder down slightly. A placeholder is moved by dragging the selection rectangle. A dotted outline is displayed as you drag to move the placeholder to show you the new location.

■ Point to the selection rectangle (not a handle) and drag the subtitle to its new location (use Figure 1-24 as a reference).

■ Clear the selection.

Your screen should be similar to Figure 1-24.

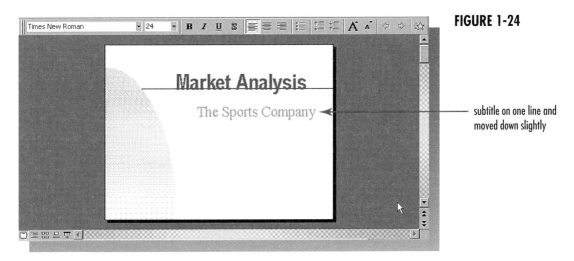

FIGURE 1-24

subtitle on one line and moved down slightly

In the next lab you will learn more about enhancing the look of your presentation.

Previewing a Presentation in Black and White

Although your presentation is in color, you want to print a black-and-white copy of the slides for the marketing department manager to review. Because shaded fills, patterns, and backgrounds that look good on the screen can make printed handouts unreadable, you want to preview how the printout will look in black and white first.

■ Click [■] Black-and-White View.

> The menu equivalent is **V**iew/**B**lack and White.

Your screen should be similar to Figure 1-25.

grayscale

switches between color and black-and-white view

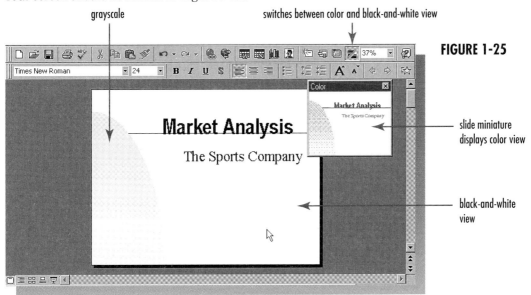

FIGURE 1-25

slide miniature displays color view

black-and-white view

You can close the slide miniature window by clicking ⊠ Close or choosing **V**iew/ Slide M**i**niature.

The slide is displayed using the default black-and-white options, and a miniature slide window displays the slide in color. The default settings display the background white, text black, and patterns in grayscale. Grayscale displays shades of gray to represent colors and shadings. The default settings can be changed to improve the appearance of the printed slides.

■ To see these options, display the slide shortcut menu and point to Black and White.

The Black-and-White submenu options are used to select different variations of the black-and-white slide. The default setting, White, creates a black-and-white slide using shades of gray and black on a white background. You like how the black-and-white version of your presentation looks.

■ Click anywhere in the work area to cancel the menu.

■ Click ▨ Black-and-White View.

The slide is displayed in color again.

Printing a Presentation

You can use the 🖨 Print button to print a presentation if you do not need to make any changes to the default print settings.

The keyboard shortcut is Ctrl + P.

You are now ready to print the slides, outline, and handouts. To print the presentation,

■ Choose **F**ile/**P**rint.

The Print dialog box on your screen should be similar to Figure 1-26.

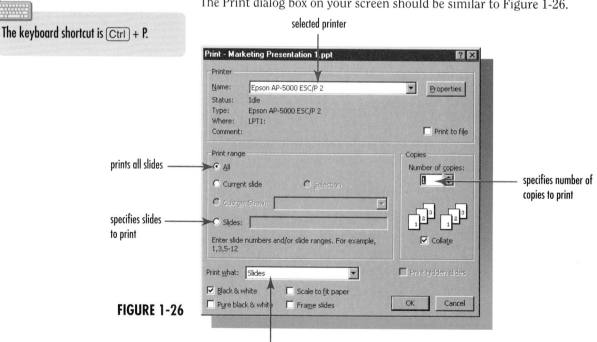

FIGURE 1-26

The Name text box in the Printer section displays the name of the selected printer. You may need to specify the printer you will be using. (Your instructor will provide the printer to select).

■   If you need to select a different printer, open the Name drop-down list and select the appropriate printer.

The Print Range settings specify which slides to print. The default setting, All, prints all the slides and Current Slide only prints the slide you are viewing. The Slides option is used to specify specific slides or a range of slides to print by entering the slide numbers in the text box.

The Copies section is used to specify the number of copies of the specified print range. The default is to print one copy. The Print What option is used to specify the type of presentation document you want to print: slides, handouts, outlines, or note pages. PowerPoint can print only one document type at a time. The default prints the slides in a presentation.

At the bottom of the dialog box, PowerPoint displays options that allow you to print color slides as black-and-white slides, to make the slide images fill the paper, and to add a frame around the slide. Black-and-white printed slides is the default. Because your manager can review the content of the presentation from the outline, you choose to print only two slides for review of the design. To print the first two slides in black and white,

> The Pure Black and White option prints your presentation in pure black and white, which hides all shades of gray.

■   Select Slides.

■   In the Slides text box, type **1,2**

■   Click [OK].

The 🖨 Printer icon appears in the status bar, indicating that the program is sending data to the Print Manager.

As soon as the slides are sent to the Print Manager program, you can tell PowerPoint to print the outline for the presentation.

> If you begin printing the second item before the printer icon is cleared, a dialog box appears advising you that another item is currently printing. The Print Status dialog box is displayed until the print job is complete.

■   Choose File/Print.

■   Select All.

■   Select Print What.

■   Select Outline View.

■   Click [OK].

Your presentation outline should be printing.

As soon as the outline is sent to the Print Manager program, you can tell PowerPoint to print the handouts for the presentation. Handouts are small printouts of each slide that can be used by the audience to follow the presentation and make notes. You can print two, three, or six slides per page. You want to print three slides per page.

■   Choose File/Print.

■   From the Print What drop-down list, select Handouts (3 slides per page).

■   Click [OK].

Documenting a File

You will save the completed presentation in a new file named Marketing Presentation 2. The original file, Marketing Presentation 1, will remain unchanged on your disk in case you want to repeat this lab later. In addition, you want to include file documentation with the file when it is saved. To do this,

- Choose File/Properties.
- Open the Summary tab if necessary.

The Summary tab text boxes are used for the following:

Option	Action
Title	Enter the presentation title. This title can be longer and more descriptive than the presentation file name.
Subject	Enter a description of the presentation's content.
Author	Enter the name of the presentation's author. By default this is the name entered when PowerPoint was installed.
Manager	Enter the name of your manager.
Company	Enter the name of your company.
Category	Enter the name of a higher level category under which you can group similar types of presentations.
Keywords	Enter words that you associate with the presentation so the Find File command can be used.
Comments	Enter any comments you feel are appropriate for the presentation.

If you press ⏎Enter, the OK button will be selected and the dialog box will close. To reopen the Summary Info dialog box, choose File/Properties.

- In the Subject text box, enter **Analysis of company sales and competition**
- In the Author text box, enter your name.

To close the dialog box and save the presentation using a new file name,

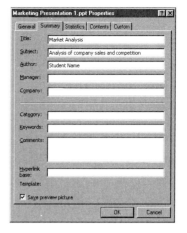

- Click **OK**.

- Choose File/Save As.

- In the File name text box, enter **Marketing Presentation 2**

- Click **Save**.

Exiting PowerPoint

You will continue to work on the presentation in the next lab. If you are ready to exit the PowerPoint program,

- Choose File/Exit.

LAB REVIEW

Key Terms

custom dictionary (PR19)	main dictionary (PR19)	serif font (PR35)
demote (PR24)	move handle (PR9)	sizing handles (PR23)
docked (PR9)	object (PR22)	slide (PR15)
Drawing toolbar (PR8)	Office Assistant (PR9)	slide show (PR31)
floating (PR9)	Outline toolbar (PR17)	Standard toolbar (PR8)
font (PR35)	placeholder (PR22)	view (PR17)
font size (PR35)	point (PR35)	work area (PR9)
footer (PR32)	promote (PR25)	
Formatting toolbar (PR8)	sans serif font (PR35)	
handouts (PR14)	selection rectangle (PR23)	

Command Summary

Command	Shortcut	Button	Action
File/**N**ew	Ctrl + N	▯	Creates a new presentation
File/**O**pen	Ctrl + O	▱	Opens selected presentation
File/**C**lose		▨	Closes presentation
File/**S**ave	Ctrl + S	▤	Saves presentation
File/Save **A**s			Saves presentation using new file name
File/**P**rint	Ctrl + P	▨	Prints presentation using default print settings
File/**P**roperties			Displays information about a file
File/E**x**it			Exits PowerPoint program

Command	Shortcut	Button	Action
Edit/Select A**ll**	Ctrl + A		Selects all slides in presentation, all text and graphics in active window, or all text in selected object
Edit/**D**elete Slide	Delete		Deletes selected slide
View/**S**lides		🗖	Switches to Slide view
View/**O**utline		☰	Switches to Outline view
View/Sli**d**e Sorter		🖴	Switches to Slide Sorter view
View/Slide Sho**w**		🖵	Runs slide show
View/**B**lack and White		🖾	Displays slides in black and white
View/Slide M**i**niature			Displays or hides a slide miniature of current slide
View/**H**eader and Footer			Specifies information that appears as headers and footers on slides, notes, outlines, and handout pages
Format/**F**ont		24 ▾	Changes font and font size
Tools/**S**pelling	F7	ᴬᴮꟼ	Spell-checks presentation

Matching

1. Match the following words with their definition or function.

1. AutoContent Wizard	_____	**a.**	displays text content of presentation only
2. Outline view	_____	**b.**	displays miniatures of all slides in presentation
3. placeholder	_____	**c.**	guides you through steps to create a presentation
4. selection rectangle	_____	**d.**	small printed copies of slides used by the audience
5. demote	_____	**e.**	indents bulleted item
6. .ppt	_____	**f.**	an electronic on-screen display of a presentation
7. Slide Sorter view	_____	**g.**	used to move and size a placeholder
8. slide show	_____	**h.**	slide elements that contain objects
9. handle	_____	**i.**	PowerPoint file name extension
10. handouts	_____	**j.**	hashed line surrounding a selected object

2. Match the following icons with their menu equivalent.

1. ᴬᴮꟼ	_____	**a.**	Outline command on View menu
2. 🗖	_____	**b.**	Slide Sorter command on View menu
3. 🖴	_____	**c.**	Print command on File menu

4. 🖫 _____ **d.** Spelling command on Tools menu

5. 🖼 _____ **e.** Font/Size command on Format menu

6. 🖥 _____ **f.** Slide command on View menu

7. 24 ▾ _____ **g.** Save command on File menu

8. 🖾 _____ **h.** Open command on File menu

9. 🖹 _____ **i.** Black and White command on View menu

10. 🖨 _____ **j.** Slide Show command on View menu

Fill-In Questions

1. In the following PowerPoint screen, several items are identified by letters. Enter the correct term for each item in the space provided.

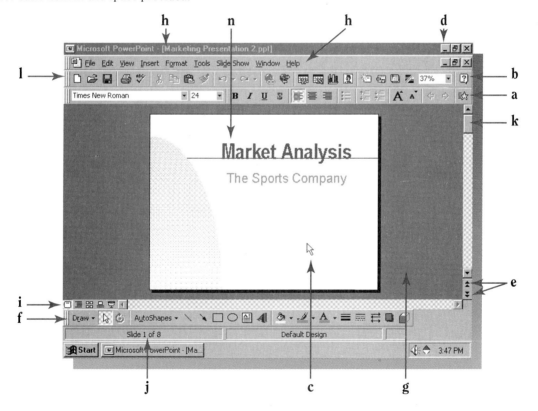

a. _____ f. _____ k. _____

b. _____ g. _____ l. _____

c. _____ h. _____ m. _____

d. _____ i. _____ n. _____

e. _____ j. _____

Hands-On Practice Exercises

Step by Step

Rating System   ☆ Easy
☆☆ Moderate
☆☆☆ Difficult

Note: All the presentations created in the following exercises will be used as a basis for the presentations created in the practice exercises in Lab 2.

1. Damion Kolb, manager of the University Recreation Center, is planning a presentation on how to prepare for a workout. To begin the presentation, complete the steps below.

a. Using the AutoContent Wizard, select Generic as the type of presentation, select Presentations as how it will be used, and select Color Overheads as the type of output for the presentation. Enter "Preparing for a Workout" in the Presentation Title text box and "University Recreation Center" in the Your name text box. Clear the Additional Information text box if necessary.

b. In Outline view, replace the sample bulleted text on slide 2 with the following:

Bullet 1:   How to have an injury-free workout

Bullet 2:   [Your Name]

c. Change the title of slide 3 to "Steps to Follow" and replace the sample bulleted text with the following:

Bullet 1:   Warm up

Bullet 2:   Stretch

Bullet 3:   Cool down

d. Switch to Slide view. Change the title of slide 4 to "Stretch" and replace the sample bulleted text with the following:

Bullet 1:   Stretch all major muscle groups

Demoted Bullet 1: Stretch and hold 10-20 seconds

Demoted Bullet 2: Move slowly and smoothly

Demoted Bullet 3: Do not bounce

Bullet 2:   Benefits

Demoted Bullet 1: Increases flexibility

Demoted Bullet 2: Helps prevent pulls and strains

e. Change the title of slide 5 to "Warm Up" and replace the sample bulleted text with the following:

Bullet 1:   Minimum of 5-10 minutes

Demoted Bullet 1: Low-level aerobic activity

Demoted Bullet 2: Slow stretches

Bullet 2:   Benefits

Demoted Bullet 1: Increases body temperature

Demoted Bullet 2: Warms up muscles

Demoted Bullet 3: Increases blood flow

f. Change the title of slide 6 to "Cool Down" and replace the sample text with the following bulleted items:

Bullet 1:   Slow stretching helps prevent muscle soreness

Bullet 2:   Minimum of 5-10 minutes slow jogging or walking

g. Switch to Slide Sorter view and delete the Real Life and What This Means slides (slides 7 and 8).

h. Switch to Slide view and change the title of slide 7 to "On Your Mark, Get Set, Go!" Size the title placeholder so the title appears on one line. Replace the sample bulleted text with the following:

Bullet 1:   The better you prepare, the more you can get out of your workout

Bullet 2:   Come to our next presentation for your personal fat analysis

i. Include the current date, the name of your school, and the slide number as a footer on all slides of the presentation.

j. Reduce the title on the title slide to 60 pt. Increase the subtitle to 40 pt and change the font to Times

New Roman. Appropriately size and move the sub-title placeholder.

k. Run the slide show.

l. Switch to Outline view. Change the order of the two bulleted items on slide 6.

m. Switch to Slide Sorter view. Switch the order of slides 4 and 5.

n. Add file summary information and save the presentation as Workout. Print the slides in black and white as handouts (three per page). Close the presentation.

You will complete this presentation in Practice Exercise 1 of Lab 2.

2. Jason Ruskey is the promotions manager for Back-Road Bikes. His job is to promote the use of off-road bikes. He is planning a presentation for a group of outdoor clubs. To begin the presentation, complete the steps below.

a. Using the AutoContent Wizard, select Generic as the type of presentation, select Presentations as how it will be used, and select on-screen presentation as the medium for the presentation. Enter "Back-Road Biking Adventures" in the Presentation Title text box and enter your name in the Your Name text box. Clear any information from the Additional Information text box.

b. In Outline view, replace the sample bulleted text on slide 2 with the following:

Bullet 1:   What's new in off-road biking

c. Replace the sample bulleted text in slide 3 with the following:

Bullet 1:   Mountain bikes

Bullet 2:   Rental locations

Bullet 3:   Trails

d. Switch to Slide view. Change the title of slide 4 to "Mountain Bikes" and replace the sample bulleted text with the following:

Bullet 1:   What are they?

Bullet 2:   Why would you want to ride one?

e. Change the title of slide 5 to "Rental Locations" and replace the sample bulleted text with the following:

Bullet 1:   American Sport

    Demoted Bullet 1: 903 Route 66

    Demoted Bullet 2: $14.99 per half day

Bullet 2:   Mountain Sports

    Demoted Bullet 1: 54 S. Mountain St.

    Demoted Bullet 2: $15.95 per half day

Bullet 3:   Western Cycles

    Demoted Bullet 1: 721 E. Maple Ave.

    Demoted Bullet 2: $20.00 per half day

f. Change the title of slide 6 to "Trails" and replace the sample bulleted text with the following:

Bullet 1:   Informational books

Bullet 2:   Maps

g. Change the title of slide 7 to "Real Life Adventure" and replace the sample bulleted text with the following:

Bullet 1:   Mud and Muck

Bullet 2:   Trail Dogs

h. Replace the sample bulleted text on slide 8 with the following:

Bullet 1:   Increased interest in the sport

Bullet 2:   Fund-raising possibilities

Bullet 3:   Group discounts

i. Change the title of Slide 9 to "Special Events." Replace the sample bulleted text on slide 9 with the following:

Bullet 1:   Day tours

Bullet 2:   Races

Bullet 3:   Overnight trips

j. Change the font and size of the title and subtitle on the title slide to improve its appearance.

k. Include the current date in the format mm/dd/yy on a footer of all slides.

l. Display slide 1 and run the slide show.

m. Switch to Outline view. Change the order of the second and third bulleted items on slides 5 and 9.

n. Switch to Slide Sorter view. Move slide 5 to follow slide 6.

o. Add file documentation and save the presentation as Back Road Biking. Print slide handouts (three per page) in black and white and the outline. Close the presentation.

You will complete this presentation in Practice Exercise 2 of Lab 2.

3. In 1999 the Parks and Recreation Department plans to build three new swimming pools. The total cost of this project is $1.2 million. However, the department does not have enough money to build the new pools. You have been asked to create a presentation that will be used to inform people about the benefits and costs of the project.

a. Using the AutoContent Wizard, select Marketing Plan as the type of presentation, select Presentations, informal meetings, handouts, as how it will be used, and select on-screen presentation as the medium for the presentation. Enter "Westwood Parks and Recreation" in the Presentation Title text box and enter your name in the Your Name text box. Clear the Additional Information text box.

b. In Outline view change the title of slide 2 to "New Pools" and replace the sample bulleted text with the following:

Bullet 1:   Why do we need three?

   Demoted Bullet 1: Population growth

   Demoted Bullet 2: School programs

   Demoted Bullet 3: Summer programs

c. Change the title of slide 3 to "Presentation Overview" and replace the sample bulleted text with the following:

Bullet 1:   Where they will be built

Bullet 2:   Benefits we can expect

Bullet 3:   Cost of the pools

d. Change the title of slide 4 to "Locations" and replace the sample bulleted text with the following:

Bullet 1:   Lake Side School

   Demoted Bullet 1: 984 S. Lake Side

Bullet 2:   Westwood Park

   Demoted Bullet 1: 832 N. Plaza Place

Bullet 3:   Baseline Park

   Demoted Bullet 1: 743 E. Thunderbird Rd.

e. Change the title of slide 5 to "Benefits" and replace the sample bulleted text with the following:

Bullet 1:   Increased pool usage

Bullet 2:   Increased revenue

Bullet 3:   Community service jobs

f. Switch to Slide view. Change the title of slide 6 to "Cost" and replace the sample bulleted text with the following:

Bullet 1:   Total needed: $1.2 million

   Demoted Bullet 1: guarantee from city: $500,000

   Demoted Bullet 2: pledged from fund-raising: $400,000

Bullet 2:   Need to raise $300,000

   Demoted Bullet 1: Telephone fund-raiser

   Next Demoted Bullet 1:   Expected amount: $100,000

   Demoted Bullet 2: 10K Fun Run

   Next Demoted Bullet 1:   Expected amount: $85,000

g. Change the title of slide 7 to "How you can help" and replace the text placeholder with the following bulleted items:

Bullet 1:   Donate money

Bullet 2:   Volunteer time with 10K Fun Run

h. Switch to Slide Sorter view and delete slides 8 through 17.

i. Increase the size of your name on slide 1.

j. Add the current date and slide number to all slides except the title slide. Run the slide show.

k. Add file documentation and save the presentation as Pool Project. Print the slides as handouts (three per page) and the outline. Close the presentation.

You will complete this presentation in Practice Exercise 3 of Lab 2.

4. Karen Miller is vice president of the Future Workers of America Association. She plans to do a presentation for college seniors on the outlook for jobs after college. To begin the presentation, complete the steps below.

Note: If the Business Plan template is not available, use Generic.

a. Using the AutoContent Wizard, select Business Plan as the type of presentation, select Presentations as how it will be used, select Color Overheads as the medium for the presentation, and enter "Degree-Rich Job-Poor" in the "Presentation Title" text box and enter your name in the "Your name" text box. Include your school name in the Additional Information text box.

b. Delete slide 2, Mission Statement.

c. Make the following changes to the slides indicated:

Slide 2   Title: Outlook

   Bullet 1:   Campus recruiting

   Bullet 2:   New hires

   Bullet 3:   Salary increases

Slide 3   Title: Campus Recruiting

   Bullet 1:   Campus visits declining

   Bullet 2:   Number of interviews

Slide 4   Title: New Hires

   Bullet 1:   New hires obtained through on-campus recruiting

   Bullet 2:   Growth in professional positions

Slide 5   Title: Salary Increases

   Bullet 1:   Changes in starting salaries

Slide 6   Title: Steps You Can Take

   Bullet 1:   Be an early bird

   Bullet 2:   Get involved and get experience

   Bullet 3:   Go to employers

   Bullet 4:   Do your homework

   Bullet 5:   Be creative

   Bullet 6:   Don't give up

Slide 7   Title: Suggestions

   Bullet 1:   Consider taking a job that does not require a degree to get a foot in the door

   Bullet 2:   Network with people who hold jobs you would like to have

   Bullet 3:   Take an internship to gain experience

   Bullet 4:   Volunteer—the more people you meet, the more likely you will find a job

d. Delete slides 8 through 11.

e. Increase the font size of the title on slide 1.

f. Run the slide show.

g. Add file documentation and save the presentation as Job Outlook. Print the slides as handouts (three per page) and the outline.

You will complete this presentation in Practice Exercise 4 of Lab 2.

On Your Own

5. As sales manager for American Cruise Incorporated, Sean Tyler is preparing a presentation to his sales associates on cruise packages around Hawaii. The company is trying to increase sales of travel packages for the third quarter.

To create this presentation, use the AutoContent Wizard and select Product/Services Overview for the type of presentation. Sean wants the presentation to include audience handouts. The presentation will be made using an on-screen presentation. Enter an appropriate title.

If necessary, improve the appearance of the title slide. Include your name on the slide. Then use the information below for the content of each slide.

Slide 2   Title: Cruise Hawaii

   Bullet 1:   Target audiences

   Bullet 2:   Destinations

Slide 3   Title: Destinations

    Bullet 1:   Historical

        Demoted Bullet 1: Ancient war god Ku

        Demoted Bullet 2: Oahu's Iolani Palace

    Bullet 2:   Scenic

        Demoted Bullet 1: Kauai's Kalalau Valley

        Demoted Bullet 2: Mt. Mauna Kea volcano

Slide 4   Title: Target Audiences

    Bullet 1:   Singles

    Bullet 2:   Families

    Bullet 3:   Groups

Slide 5   Title: Benefits

    Bullet 1:   Year-round travel dates available

    Bullet 2:   Reduced rates for cruise departures in July and August

    Bullet 3:   Find exotic destinations without leaving the country

Slide 6   Title: Action Plan

    Bullet 1:   Create brochures for travel agents

    Bullet 2:   Advertise in travel magazines

    Bullet 3:   Make group presentations

Delete slide 7. Run the slide show. Change the order of the first and third bulleted items on slide 5. Move slide 3 to follow slide 4. Add "Unbeatable Combination of Service and Great Prices" as bullet 4 on slide 5. Run the slide show again. Add file documentation and save the presentation as Cruise Promotion. Print the slides as handouts (three per page) and the outline.

You will complete this presentation in Practice Exercise 5 of Lab 2.

6. You work in an HMO's regional offices in the Patient Relations Department. One of your responsibilities is to prepare presentations to be given at the local HMO offices. Your current project is to prepare a presentation on weight control. After researching the recent literature and consulting with several experts on the topic, you have compiled the following information for managing your weight.

The experts all agree that the only way to maintain a healthy weight is by eating a healthy diet and getting regular exercise.

The following tips will help you attain a well-balanced, healthy diet:

    Eat more low-fat, low-cholesterol foods, such as fruits, vegetables, rice, and pasta. These foods are high in fiber and complex carbohydrates and are filling without being high in fat.

    Bake, broil, or steam your food instead of frying.

    Use oil for cooking instead of butter or margarine. Canola, safflower, and olive oils are good choices.

    Trim the fat from meat, remove the skin from chicken, and add more fish to your diet.

    Choose low-fat products. Milk, cheese, mayonnaise, and salad dressing are all available in low-fat or fat-free varieties.

    Eat smaller portions at a slower pace to avoid overeating.

    Try not to eat after 7 P.M., so your body has time to digest your food before you go to sleep.

Regular exercise is just as important as watching what you eat. Exercise burns fat and develops muscles. It also increase the metabolism. Here are some tips about adding physical activity to your daily routine.

- Take stairs instead of the elevator.
- Get off the bus at an earlier stop and walk the rest of the way.
- Walk your dog.
- Start out slowly and increase the level of exercise gradually.
- Choose an activity you enjoy.
- Consult your physician before you begin an exercise routine.
- Attend an aerobics class.
- Work out with a friend.

Use the information presented above and any other knowledge you may have on this topic to create an on-screen presentation using the AutoContent Wizard and selecting the Project Overview presentation type. Include your name on the title slide. Print the first slide and the presentation outline. Save the presentation as Weight Control.

7. Create a presentation based on a lecture that could be or has been given in one of your classes. Use the AutoContent Wizard to create the presentation. Select the Generic presentation type. Add titles and bullets to the slides. Save the presentation and print the outline and slides.

You will complete this presentation in Practice Exercise 5 of Lab 3.

Creating a Presentation

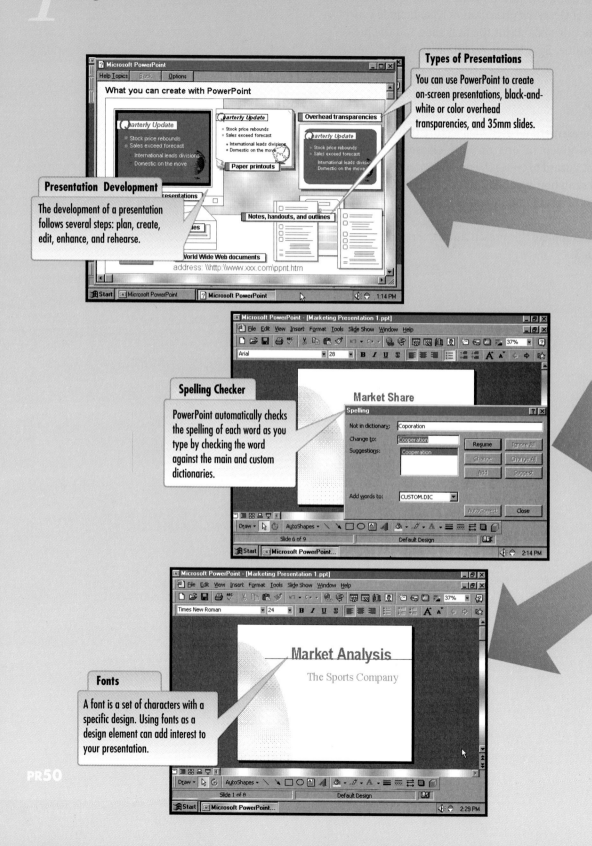

Types of Presentations

You can use PowerPoint to create on-screen presentations, black-and-white or color overhead transparencies, and 35mm slides.

Presentation Development

The development of a presentation follows several steps: plan, create, edit, enhance, and rehearse.

Spelling Checker

PowerPoint automatically checks the spelling of each word as you type by checking the word against the main and custom dictionaries.

Fonts

A font is a set of characters with a specific design. Using fonts as a design element can add interest to your presentation.

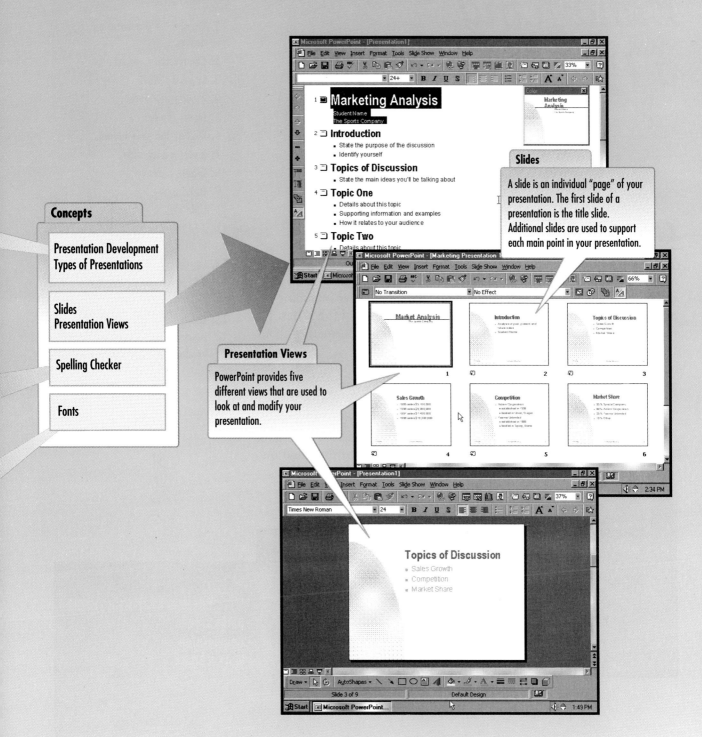

Concepts

Presentation Development
Types of Presentations

Slides
Presentation Views

Spelling Checker

Fonts

Slides

A slide is an individual "page" of your presentation. The first slide of a presentation is the title slide. Additional slides are used to support each main point in your presentation.

Presentation Views

PowerPoint provides five different views that are used to look at and modify your presentation.

Enhancing a Presentation

COMPETENCIES

After completing this lab, you will know how to:

1. Change the presentation design.
2. Change the color scheme.
3. Expand slides.
4. Modify attributes.
5. Insert clip art.
6. Change the slide layout.
7. Insert a new slide.
8. Create a chart.
9. Draw a box.
10. Hide slides.
11. Add transition and build effects.
12. Control a slide show.
13. Add freehand annotations.
14. Create speaker notes.
15. Check the presentation.
16. Print selected slides and handouts.

CASE STUDY

You have discussed the presentation with the marketing department manager, who suggests that you include graphs to illustrate the data on sales and market share. It was also suggested that you consider including art and other graphic features to enhance the appearance of the slides. Finally, you have been asked to include some additional information about the competition.

PowerPoint 97 gives you the design and production capabilities to create a first-class on-screen presentation. These features include artist-designed layouts and color schemes that give your presentation a professional appearance. In addition, you can add your own personal touches by modifying text attributes, incorporating art or graphics, and including animation to add impact, interest, and excitement to your presentation.

Several slides from your completed presentation are shown below.

Concept Overview

The following concepts will be introduced in this lab:

1. Design Templates   Design templates are professionally created slide designs that can be applied to a presentation.

2. Attributes   An attribute is a feature associated with an object or text that can be enhanced using drawing tools and menu commands.

3. Master   A master is a special slide or page on which the formatting for all slides or pages in your presentation is defined.

4. Graphics   Graphics are objects such as charts, drawings, and pictures that you can add to a presentation to provide visual interest or clarify data.

5. AutoLayout   PowerPoint includes 24 predefined slide layouts, called AutoLayouts, that are used to control the placement of objects on a slide.

6. Charts   Charts, visual representations of numeric data, are used to help an audience grasp the impact of your data more quickly.

7. Special Effects   Special effects such as slide transitions and builds are used to enhance the on-screen presentation.

Part 1

Changing the Presentation Design

You have updated the content to include the additional information on the competition and are now ready to make several changes to improve the overall appearance of the presentation.

- Load PowerPoint 97.

- Put your data disk in drive A (or the appropriate drive for your system).

- Open the file Marketing Presentation 3 from your data disk.

- Replace Student Name on slide 2 with your name.

- Switch to Slide Sorter view.

Slide 6 contains the additional information on the competition.

You will be using many PowerPoint features to enhance the presentation. To make it easier to access these features, you will use the Common Tasks toolbar.

- Display the Common Tasks toolbar.

- Move it to a corner of the work area.

Select the Common Tasks toolbar from the toolbar Shortcut menu.

Your screen should be similar to Figure 2-1.

FIGURE 2-1

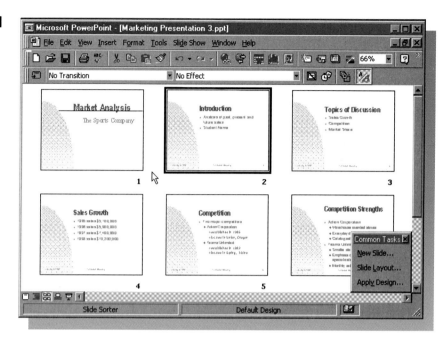

This toolbar consists of three buttons that are frequently used to modify a presentation.

Although you are satisfied with the presentation's basic content and organization, you want to change its style and appearance by applying a different design template.

Concept 1: Design Templates

Design templates are professionally created slide designs that can be applied to your presentation. They contain color schemes, custom formatting, background designs, styled fonts, and other layout and design elements that have been created by artists. There are more than 100 design templates from which you can select to quickly give your presentations a professional appearance. Selecting a design template changes all slides in your presentation to match the selected template design. This ensures that your presentation has a consistent look throughout.

To change the design template,

The menu equivalent is F**o**rmat/Appl**y** Design.

■   Click   Appl**y** Design... .

The Apply Design dialog box on your screen should be similar to Figure 2-2.

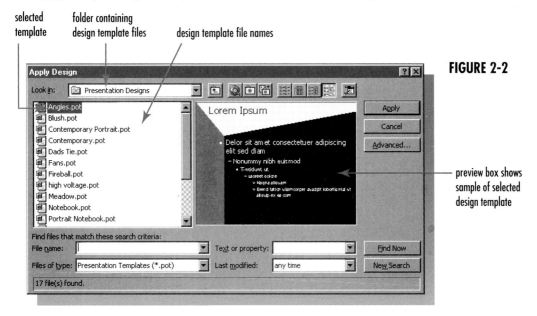

selected template

folder containing design template files

design template file names

FIGURE 2-2

preview box shows sample of selected design template

The large list box on the left displays the names of the design templates located in the Presentation Designs folder. When a design template file name is selected, the preview box displays a sample of the colors, fonts, and designs for the selected design. The first design template in the list, Angles, is the selected and displayed design template.

The file extension for PowerPoint design templates is .pot.

■ Select several design templates and view the samples in the preview box.

Click on the design file name to select it.

After previewing the templates, you decide to use the Blush template for your presentation.

■ Double-click Blush.

Your screen should be similar to Figure 2-3.

FIGURE 2-3

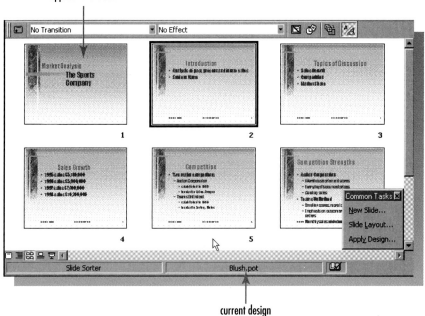

The design has been applied all slides in the presentation. The status bar displays the name of the current design.

Changing the Color Scheme

As you look at the new design style, you feel the color is not very powerful. To make your presentation more lively, you decide to try a different color scheme. Each design template has several alternative color schemes from which you can choose. To see the color schemes that are available for the Blush template,

- ■ Choose F*o*rmat/Slide *C*olor Scheme.
- ■ If necessary, open the Standard tab.

The Color Scheme dialog box on your screen should be similar to Figure 2-4.

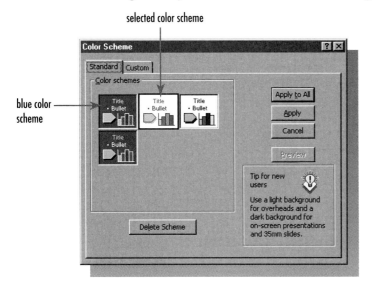

selected color scheme

blue color scheme

FIGURE 2-4

The four color schemes for the Blush design template are displayed. The color scheme with the white background is selected. Each color scheme consists of eight coordinated colors that are applied to different slide elements. Using pre-defined color schemes gives your presentation a professional and consistent look. To see how the pink color scheme would look,

- Select the pink color scheme option (first design, second row).

- Click Preview .

- Move the dialog box so you can see the upper row of slides in the work area.

Your screen should be similar to Figure 2-5.

preview of selected color screen

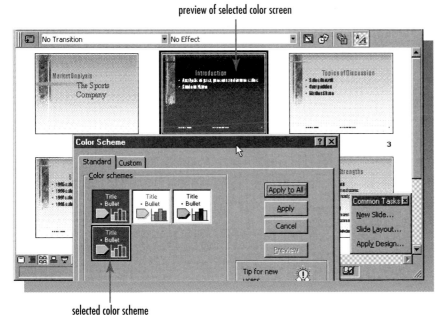

FIGURE 2-5

selected color scheme

The current slide is displayed in the selected color scheme. Although you like this color scheme, you think the background is too dark, and you want to change the standard colors of the template design.

■ Open the Custom tab.

The Color Scheme dialog box on your screen should be similar to Figure 2-6.

FIGURE 2-6

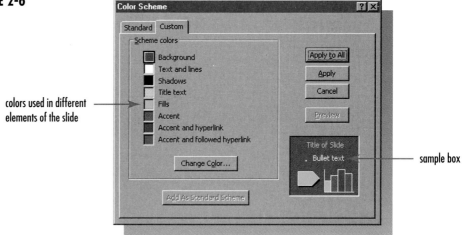

colors used in different elements of the slide

sample box

The Scheme Colors area of the dialog box shows you the eight colors that are applied to different elements of the template design. The sample box shows how the selected colors are used in a slide. The option to change the background color is selected by default. To select a different color for the background,

■ Click Change Color...

The Background Color dialog box on your screen should be similar to Figure 2-7.

FIGURE 2-7

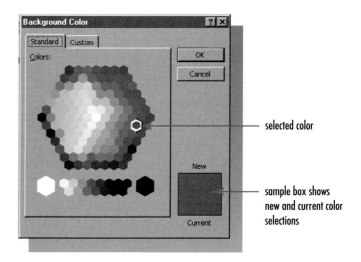

selected color

sample box shows new and current color selections

The dialog box displays a palette of standard colors. The current color of the background is selected. The sample box shows the new color in the upper half and the current color in the lower half. Because you have not yet selected a new color, only one color is displayed. To see how the lighter shade of the same color will look,

■ Select the color two to the left of the current selected color.

As you can see in the New and Current sample boxes, the new color is much brighter and gives the slide the look you want. You can apply the different color scheme to just one slide in your presentation or to all the slides. To apply the new color to all the slides,

■ Click [OK] .

■ Click [Apply to All] .

■ To see how the changes you have made look when the slide is full screen, run the slide show.

> The same procedure is used to change the colors of any other elements on the template.

Expanding Slides

As you looked at the slides, you noticed that slide 6 with the new information on the competition contains too much information. You want to break the information into separate slides. You could do this in Outline view by changing the levels of heads to create two separate slides. Another way is to use the Expand Slide feature to create separate slides for each paragraph on the slide. To use this feature,

■ Select slide 6.

■ Choose Tools/Expand slide.

■ If necessary, scroll the window to see slides 7 and 8.

Your screen should be similar to Figure 2-8.

FIGURE 2-8

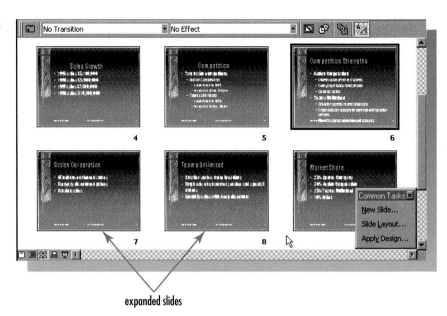

expanded slides

Two new slides, 7 and 8, have been created, one for each paragraph in slide 6. Slide 6 is unchanged.

■ Since you no longer need slide 6, delete it.

Modifying Attributes

Also while viewing the slide show, you noticed many slides had a lot of blank space. You want to reduce the amount of blank space by increasing the font size on all the slides. You also think the slide appearance could be improved by using different effects to enhance the text attributes.

Concept 2: Attributes

An **attribute** is a feature associated with an object or text that can be enhanced using drawing tools and menu commands. Text attributes can be enhanced by applying different styles and effects to the text to add impact or interest. Fonts and font size are two basic text attributes. Other text attributes are text color and style. **Style** refers to text attributes such as bold and italics. You can also apply special effects such as shadows and embossed text effects to text. Object attributes that can be manipulated are the object's line style, fill, shadow, color, and shape. Examples of text attributes and object attributes that have been enhanced are shown below.

Text   **Object**

In a well-designed presentation, the use of different attributes enhances the presentation. However, too many different attributes may clutter and detract from the content rather than enhance the presentation.

First you will eliminate some of the blank space on the slides by increasing the font size. Although you can change each slide individually as you did in Lab 1, you can make the change much faster to all the slides by changing the slide master.

Concept 3: Master

A **master** is a special slide or page on which the formatting for all slides or pages in your presentation is defined. Each component of a presentation—title slide, slides, note pages, and handout pages—has a corresponding master. The master contains formatted placeholders for the titles, main text, footnotes, background elements, and so on that appear on each associated slide or page. Any changes you make to a master affect all slides or pages associated with that master. The four masters are described below.

Master	Function
Slide Master	Defines the format and placement for the title and body text as well as the background art for each slide in a presentation.
Title Master	Defines the format and placement of titles and text for slides that use the title layout.
Handout Master	Defines the format and placement of the slide image, text, headers and footers, and other elements that are to appear on every audience handout.
Notes Master	Defines the format and placement of the slide image, note text, headers and footers, and other elements that are to appear on all speaker notes.

If you modify the text color, font style, or size for slide titles on the slide master, all slides in the presentation will change accordingly. Likewise, if you add a graphic such as a company logo to the slide master, it appears on every slide. However, if you modify the format or layout of the title master, only those slides you have designated as title slides in your presentation will change. When you apply a new design template to a presentation, all slides and masters are updated to those of the new design template.

You can create slides that differ from the master by changing the format and placement of elements in the individual slide rather than on the master. For example, when you change the font of a title on a single slide, the slide master is not affected. Only the individual slide reflects the change, making it unique. If you have created a unique slide, the elements you changed on that slide retain their uniqueness even if you later make changes to the slide master, including changing the design template.

Using the master to modify or add elements to a presentation ensures consistency and saves time.

Each master is displayed in its own view. To display the slide master,

- Choose View/Master/Slide Master.

You also can hold down ⟨⇧ Shift⟩ and click the ▢ Slide View button to display the slide master.

PRESENTATION

Your slide master should be similar to Figure 2-9.

FIGURE 2-9

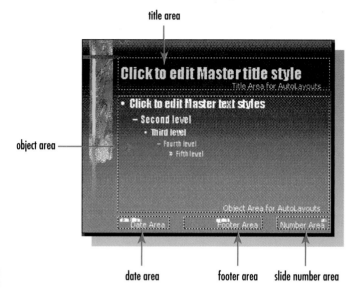

title area

object area

date area   footer area   slide number area

The Master toolbar may also be displayed.

The slide master consists of five placeholders that control the appearance of all slides. Each placeholder displays sample text to show you how changes you make in these areas will appear. First you will increase the size of the title text from 44 to 54 points.

■ Click on the title area.

■ Use the [44 ▼] Font Size button to increase the font size to 54.

Next you want to change the title text color. Color is one of many attributes that can be modified to enhance the appearance of text or objects.

■ Click [A ▼] Font Color.

The More Font Colors option opens the standard color palette.

Thirteen colors that are coordinated with your selected color scheme are displayed in the drop-down list.

■ Select lime green.

Your slide should be similar to Figure 2-10.

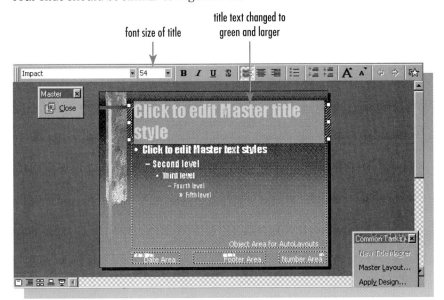

FIGURE 2-10

Next you want to increase the size of the bulleted text in the object area.

■ Click the first-level head in the object area and increase the font size from 32 to 40.

■ In a similar manner, increase the font size of the second-level bulleted text from 28 to 32.

Your slide master should be similar to Figure 2-11.

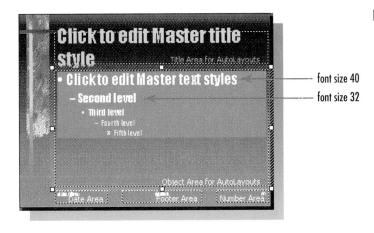

FIGURE 2-11

To see how the changes you have made to the slide master affected the slides,

■ Click 🔠 Slide Sorter View.

The point size and color changes to the title appear in all slides. The changes to the two levels of bulleted text are reflected in all slides containing those level heads.

You think the Competition slide (slide 5), which contains a lot of text, would look better if the font of the first- and second-level bulleted text was a smaller size.

■ Display slide 5 in Slide view.

■ Select the first-level bulleted text.

You will decrease the font size to 36 points using the 🔲 Decrease Font Size button. This button will decrease the point size of the selected text in 10 percent increments.

■ Click 🔲 Decrease Font Size.

Your screen should be similar to Figure 2-12.

The ⒶIncrease Font Size button will increase the point size by 10 percent.

The menu equivalent is F**o**rmat/**F**ont/ **S**ize/32.

FIGURE 2-12

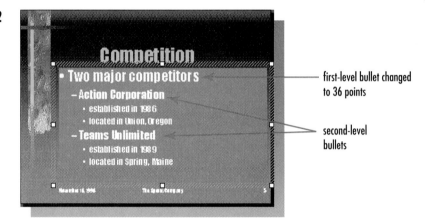

■ In a similar manner, reduce the size of the two second-level bulleted items to 28 points.

The changes you have made to this slide affect the current slide only, making it a unique slide in the presentation. The slide master is not changed. If you now changed the second-level bulleted text on the slide master, the second-level text on this slide would not be affected, because changes made to an individual slide override the master slide.

Next you want to enhance the appearance of the title slide by adding a shadow and italics to the title and changing the subtitle text to a different color with a shadow using the title master.

■ Display slide 1.

■ Hold down ⇧Shift and click 🔲 Slide View.

■ Click the master title text placeholder.

The menu equivalent is **V**iew/**M**aster/ **T**itle Master.

Your screen should be similar to Figure 2-13.

title font style   title font size

title text color

FIGURE 2-13

Notice that the title master has a slightly different appearance from the title slide in your presentation. This is because you modified the title slide in the previous lab, making it a unique slide. The unique changes you made to that slide (the font, style, point size, and location of the subtitle) were not changed to those in the title master of the Blush design template. The attributes that are applied to the title text are Impact, 54 points, with a text color of lime green. The toolbar buttons indicate these settings are in use.

- Click **I** Italic.

- Click **S** Shadow.

- In a similar manner, apply italics and a shadow to the subtitle text and change the text color to orange (first color, second row).

To see how the title slide looks with the changes you have made,

- Click **☐** Slide View.

You feel the subtitle is too large and close to the title.

- Select the subtitle text and reduce the font size to 48.

- Increase the size of the placeholder so the subtitle is displayed on a single line.

- Move the subtitle to the location shown in Figure 2-14.

- Clear the selection.

A depressed button means the feature is on.

The menu equivalent is F**o**rmat/**F**ont/F**o**nt Style/Italic/Sh**a**dow.

PRESENTATION

Your screen should be similar to Figure 2-14.

title text with shadow and italics

FIGURE 2-14

subtitle text with shadow and in new color

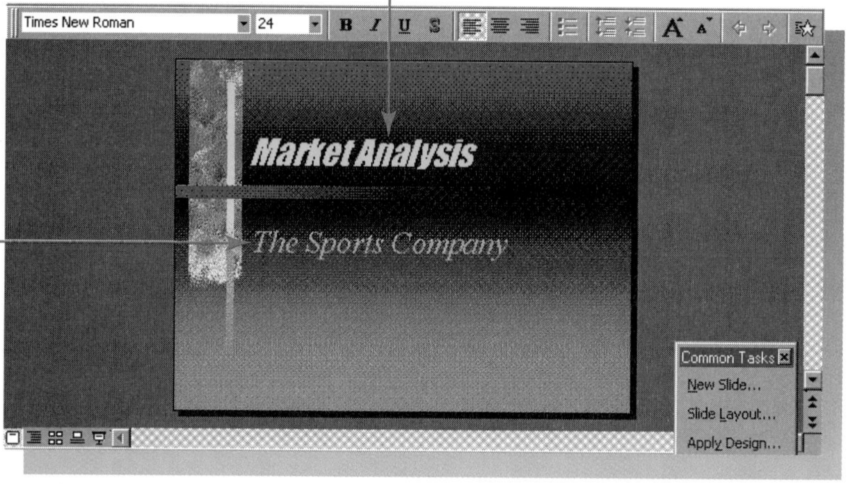

Inserting Clip Art

As suggested by the marketing department manager, you decide to add several graphic elements to the slides.

Concept 4: Graphics

Graphics are objects such as charts, drawings, pictures, and scanned photographs you can add to a presentation to provide visual interest or clarify data. Drawing objects, pictures, and clip art are all types of graphic objects.

A **drawing object** consists of shapes such as lines and boxes that can be created using the Drawing toolbar. A **picture** is an illustration created by combining lines, arcs, circles, and other shapes. It is commonly created using a graphic application such as Paint. You can also draw a picture using the features on the Drawing toolbar. Pictures created using other applications are stored as graphic files. **Clip art** refers to a collection of graphics that usually is bundled with a software application. You also can purchase clip art packages to add to your collection.

As you add objects to a document, they automatically stack in layers. When objects overlap in the layer, the top object covers a portion of objects beneath it, creating an overlapping stack. Many times this is the effect you want to achieve. Other times, however you do not want the layers to overlap. You can move and size graphic objects and change their stacking order to suit your needs. Once graphic files are inserted into a presentation, they are saved with the presentation.

Graphics files commonly have file extensions such as .wmf, .bmp, .tif, .pcx, .wpg, .pic, and .cgm.

The menu equivalent is Insert/Picture/ Clip Art.

First you will add a clip art drawing to the second slide.

- Move to slide 2.

- Click 🔲 Insert Clip Art.

The Microsoft Clip Gallery 3.0 dialog box on your screen should be similar to Figure 2-15.

clip art categories   clip art drawings

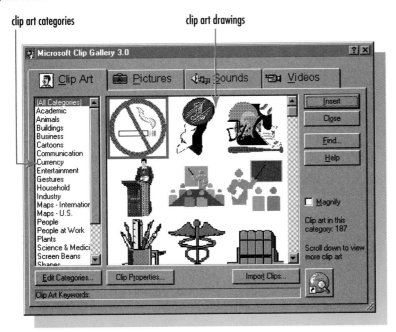

FIGURE 2-15

The categories and images in your dialog box may be different from those in Figure 2-15.

The Categories list box lists all categories of clip art images. Because the selected category is All Categories, the gallery displays images of all the clip art drawings that are available. You want to add an image to slide 2 showing leadership. To help find an image that might reflect this characteristic,

■ Click  .

The Find Clip dialog box on your screen should be similar to Figure 2-16.

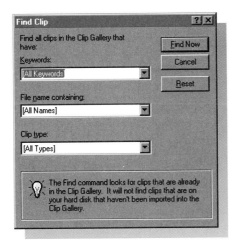

FIGURE 2-16

Each clip art image has been named and assigned several keywords that describe the content of the image. You can search for clip art by entering a keyword, or by the file name or file type. To search using a keyword,

- ▪ In the Keywords text box, type **Leadership**

- ▪ Click Find Now .

After a few moments, all clip art images that have "leadership" in their description are displayed.

Refer to Figure 2-17 to help you find the correct clip art image.

- ▪ Select

- ▪ Click Insert .

Your slide should be similar to Figure 2-17.

FIGURE 2-17

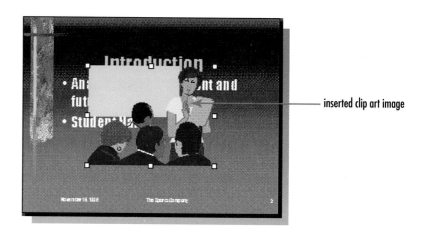

inserted clip art image

Your image may come in a different size than shown here.

The selected clip art image is displayed on the slide, but it is not the size you want and overlaps the bulleted text. Notice that the image is displayed with handles, indicating that it is a selected object. The Picture toolbar is also automatically displayed whenever a graphic object is selected. Its buttons (identified below) are used to modify and enhance the picture object.

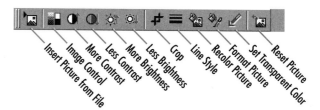

You move and size objects just like selected placeholders.

- ▪ Move and size the image until your slide is similar to Figure 2-18.
- ▪ Clear the selection.

Your slide should be similar to Figure 2-18.

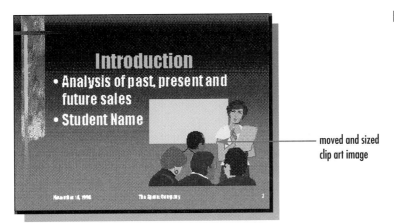

FIGURE 2-18

moved and sized
clip art image

Changing Slide Layout

You would also like to add a clip art drawing to slide 10. Before inserting the clip art, you would like to change the layout of this slide to make space for the clip art object. To do this,

- Display slide 10.

- Click Slide Layout... .

The Slide Layout dialog box on your screen should be similar to Figure 2-19.

> The menu equivalent is F**o**rmat/Slide L**a**yout.

selected layout

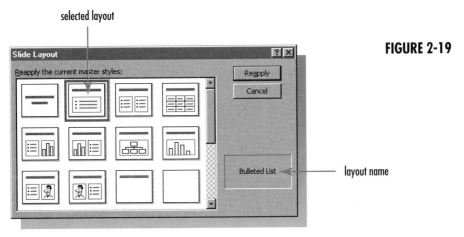

FIGURE 2-19

layout name

The current layout, Bulleted List, is selected. You want to change the layout to a style that is designed to accommodate both text and clip art.

> ## Concept 5: AutoLayout
>
> PowerPoint includes 24 predefined slide layouts called **AutoLayouts** that are used to control the placement of objects on a slide. For example, there is a layout that includes placeholders for a title and bulleted text, and another with placeholders for a title, text, and clip art. The title and text placeholders follow the formatting of the slide master for your presentation. You can move, resize, or reformat the layouts so they vary from the slide master.
>
> You also can change the layout of an existing slide. If the new layout does not include placeholders for objects that are already on your slide (for example, if you created a chart and the new layout does not include a chart placeholder), you do not lose the information. All objects remain on the slide, and you can rearrange them to fit the new layout.
>
> To make creating slides easy, use the predefined layouts. The layouts help you keep your presentation format consistent and, therefore, more professional.

To apply a new layout to the current slide,

- Select ▦ Text & Clip Art (first slide in third row).

- Choose [Apply].

Your slide should be similar to Figure 2-20.

FIGURE 2-20

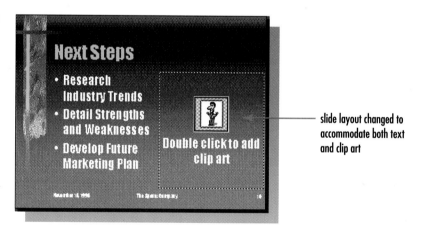

slide layout changed to accommodate both text and clip art

All the text has moved into the bullet placeholder on the left side of the slide, and a clip art placeholder has been inserted on the right. You are ready to add a new clip art image.

- Double-click the clip art placeholder.

- From the Categories list box, select Shapes.

- Double-click ⇶.

> Refer to Figure 2-21 to help you locate the correct clip art image.

Your screen should be similar to Figure 2-21.

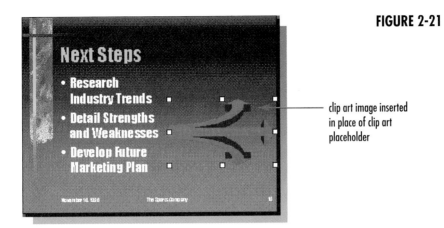

FIGURE 2-21

clip art image inserted
in place of clip art
placeholder

By changing the slide layout before inserting the clip art, you do not need to adjust
the size of the clip art and the image does not overlap any text on the slide.

Now you want to change the color of the graphic to coordinate with the
other slide colors.

■ Click [icon] Recolor Picture.

> Recolor Picture is located on the
> Picture toolbar.

The Recolor Picture dialog box on your screen should be similar to Figure 2-22.

maroon shadow

FIGURE 2-22

red fill color

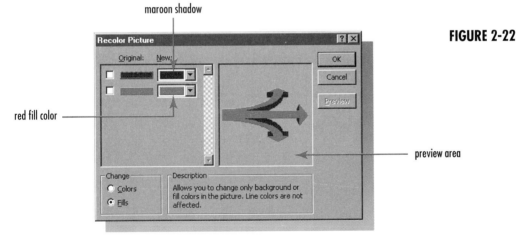

preview area

■ Change the maroon shadow to dark green and the red fill color
to lime green.

The preview area changes to match your selection. To see
how the new colors look on your slide,

■ Click | Preview |.

■ Move the Recolor Picture dialog box out of the way to see the graphic on the slide.

■ Click | OK |.

■ Deselect the picture.

Note: If you are ending your session now, save the presentation as Final Marketing Presentation and exit PowerPoint. When you begin Part 2, open this file.

Part 2

Inserting a New Slide

During your discussion with the marketing department manager, it was suggested that you graphically illustrate the data on sales and market share shown in slide 4 and 9. To include this information in the presentation for the sales data, first you will insert a new slide after slide 4.

- Display slide 4.

- Click New Slide... .

> The menu equivalent is **I**nsert/**N**ew Slide, and the keyboard shortcut is [Ctrl] + M.

The slide AutoLayout options are displayed in the New Slide dialog box. You want the slide to include a bulleted item above a graph of the sales data. Although there are layouts that include both text and graphs, these layouts place the text and graph side by side on the slide. Because you want the bulleted text to appear above the graph, you will select the Bulleted List AutoLayout and then add the graphed data to the slide.

- Double-click [icon] Bulleted List.

A new slide, 5, with title and bullet placeholders is inserted after slide 4. The new slide has the same design settings as the master slide.

- Replace the sample title text with **Sales Growth**

- Replace the bulleted item sample text with **Sales doubled in 4 years**

Your slide should be similar to Figure 2-23.

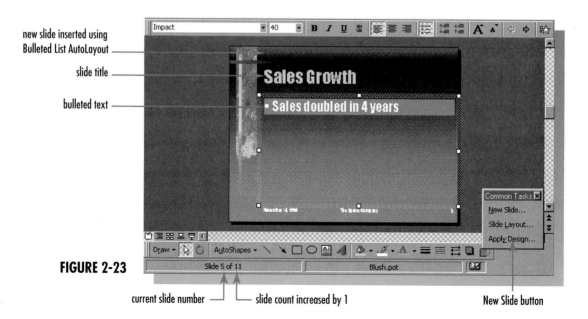

new slide inserted using Bulleted List AutoLayout

slide title

bulleted text

FIGURE 2-23

current slide number — slide count increased by 1 — New Slide button

Creating a Chart

The new slide will visually display the data from slide 4 in the form of a chart.

Concept 6: Charts

A **chart**, also called a **graph**, is a visual representation of numeric data. When you are presenting data to an audience, they will grasp the impact of your data more quickly if you present it as a chart. PowerPoint can produce 14 types of charts with many different formats for each type. Each type of chart represents the data differently and has a different purpose. It is important to select the type of chart that will provide the right emphasis to support your presentations. The basic chart types are shown below.

Type of Chart	Description
Area chart	Shows the relative importance of a value over time by emphasizing the area under the curve created by each data series.
Bar chart	Displays the categories vertically and the values horizontally, placing more emphasis on comparisons and less on time. Stacked-bar charts are often used to compare values and totals by stacking bars on top of one another.
Column chart	Similar to a bar chart, except categories are organized horizontally and values vertically.
Line chart	Shows changes in data over time, emphasizing time and rate of change rather than the amount of change.
Pie chart	Shows the relationship of each value in a data series to the series as a whole. Each slice of the pie represents a single value in the series.

Most charts are made up of several basic parts.

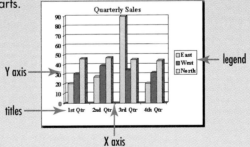

Part	Description
X axis	The bottom boundary of the chart, also called the category axis, is used to label the data being charted; the label may be, for example, a point in time or a category.
Y axis	The left boundary of the chart, also called the value axis, is a numbered scale whose numbers are determined by the data used in the chart. Each bar in the chart represents a data value. In pie charts there are no axes. Instead, the data that is charted is displayed as slices in a circle or pie.
Legend	A brief description of the symbols used in a chart.
Titles	Descriptive text used to explain the content of the chart.

The menu equivalent is <u>I</u>nsert/C<u>h</u>art.

You can also insert a chart created in Excel.

To insert a chart, the Graph application within PowerPoint is used.

■   Click [icon] Insert Chart.

Your screen should be similar to Figure 2-24.

FIGURE 2-24

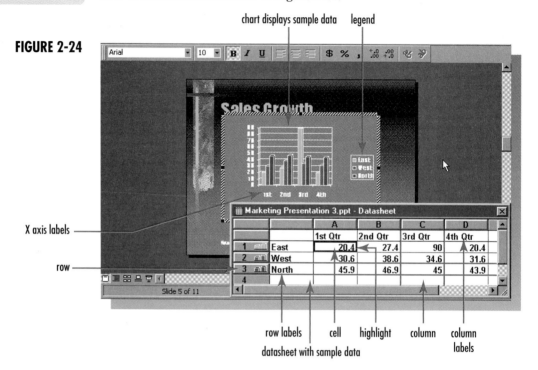

A datasheet containing sample data is displayed in the Datasheet window, and a bar chart using the sample data from the datasheet is displayed in the slide. The **datasheet** is a table consisting of rows and columns. The intersection of a row and column creates a **cell** in which text or data is entered. The cell that is surrounded by the border, called the **highlight**, is the selected cell. The selected cell is the cell you can work in.

Drag the Datasheet window title bar to move the window.

■   If necessary, move the Datasheet window to the bottom of the work area.

To create a chart that displays the sales growth for the four years, you need to replace the sample data in the datasheet with the actual sales data. In addition to displaying sample data, the datasheet also contains placeholders for the row labels, which are used as the legend in the chart, and for the column labels, which are used as X-axis labels. First you will replace the Qtr labels with the years from slide 4. To do this you need to select the cell you want to change by moving the highlight. To move the highlight, click on the cell you want to move to or use the directional keys.

The sample entries are automatically replaced when you enter new data.

■   Select the cell containing 1st Qtr.

■ Type **1995**

■ Press →.

■ Type **1996**

■ Press →.

■ In a similar manner, change 3rd Qtr and 4th Qtr to 1997 and 1998, respectively.

The chart is updated to reflect the changes as they are made to the datasheet. The years appear along the X axis. Next you will replace the East label with Sales and enter the sales data. The amounts will be entered in millions of dollars. For example, $5,100,000 will be entered as 5.1.

■ Move to the cell containing East.

■ Type **Sales**

■ Press →.

■ Type **5.1**

■ Press →.

Notice that the datasheet displays the column letters A through D and row numbers 1 through 4. Each cell has a unique name consisting of a column letter followed by a row number. For example, cell A1 is the intersection of column A and row 1.

■ Enter the rest of the data in the following cells of the datasheet:

Cell	Entry
B1	5.9
C1	7.4
D1	10.2

The chart reflects the change in sales data. Finally, you need to remove the remaining two rows of sample data.

■ Click the row heading to the left of the West label and drag down to select row 3.

■ Press Delete.

Your screen should be similar to Figure 2-25.

FIGURE 2-25

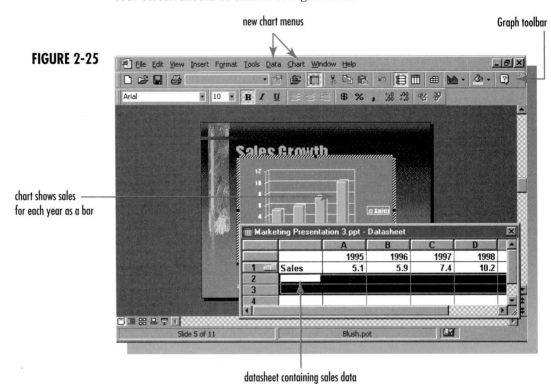

new chart menus

Graph toolbar

chart shows sales for each year as a bar

datasheet containing sales data

The sample data in rows 2 and 3 are erased, and the bar chart now displays the single set of sales data. After considering the bar chart, you feel this type of chart will not represent the sales data very well. You want to show the importance of sales over time from 1995 to 1998. You feel that an area chart would show this best. The Graph application also includes its own menus and toolbar buttons (identified below) designed to modify charts.

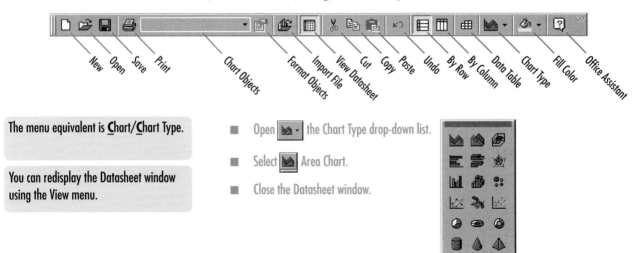

New   Open   Save   Print   Chart Objects   Format Objects   Import File   View Datasheet   Cut   Copy   Paste   Undo   By Row   By Column   Data Table   Chart Type   Fill Color   Office Assistant

The menu equivalent is **Chart/Chart Type.**

You can redisplay the Datasheet window using the View menu.

- Open the Chart Type drop-down list.

- Select Area Chart.

- Close the Datasheet window.

Your slide should be similar to Figure 2-26.

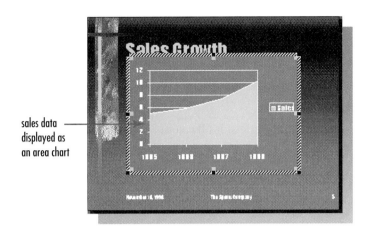

sales data
displayed as
an area chart

FIGURE 2-26

The Graph application is still active and the Graph menu and toolbar are still displayed, so you can continue to edit the graph. Because the chart contains only one set of data, you do not need a legend. To delete the legend from the chart,

■ Click on the legend.

■ Press Delete.

The chart clearly shows how sales have increased over the last four years. However, it overlaps and conceals the bulleted text.

■ Size and move the chart until it fits below the bulleted item.

■ Clear the selection.

Your slide should be similar to Figure 2-27.

The **C**hart/Chart **O**ptions/Legend/**S**how Legend command hides and displays a chart legend.

FIGURE 2-27

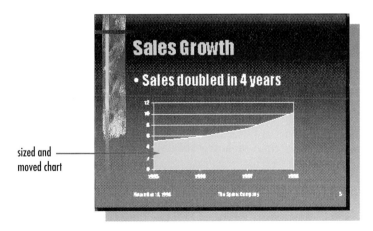

sized and
moved chart

The Graph application is closed and you are returned to PowerPoint.

Double-clicking on the chart will open the Graph application again.

PRESENTATION

Drawing a Box

To help define the chart space, you decide to draw a box around it using the Rectangle Tool on the Drawing toolbar.

- ■ Click ▢ Rectangle.

- ■ Position the mouse pointer at the top left corner of the chart, and drag to create an outline box around the chart.

The graph is covered by the default fill color of the box you created. To remove the fill color,

> If your border line is not displayed, click and select Automatic.

- ■ Open the ◇ ▾ Fill Color drop-down list.

- ■ Click ⬛ No Fill ⬛.

> The menu equivalent is F**o**rmat/Colors and Li**n**es/**C**olor/No Fill.

- ■ Clear the selection.

Your slide should be similar to Figure 2-28.

FIGURE 2-28

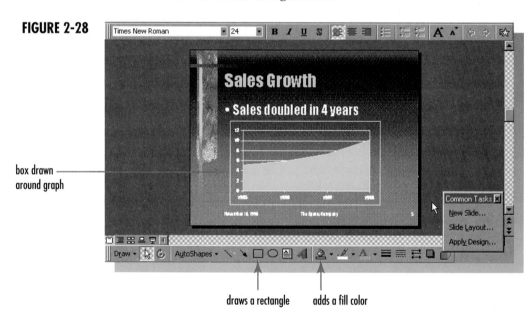

box drawn around graph

draws a rectangle   adds a fill color

Inserting a Pie Chart

Next you want to add a chart on a new slide following slide 9 to represent the data on market share.

- ■ Insert a new slide after slide 9 using the ▦ Text and Chart AutoLayout.

- ■ Replace the sample title text with **Market Share**.

■ Add the following two bulleted items:

Two major competitors

The Sports Company share is 35%

You want the graph to show the relative size of each company's market share to the total market. To do this, you will use a pie chart.

■ Double-click the chart placeholder.

■ Change the chart type to a pie chart.

■ Update the datasheet with the data shown in the datasheet below.

■ Delete the East label.

■ Delete rows 2 and 3.

		A	B	C	D
		Sports	Action	Teams	Other
1	Pie 1	35	30	25	10
2					
3					
4					

Marketing Presentation 3.ppt - Datasheet

The datasheet now contains all the information for the pie chart.

■ Close the Datasheet window and clear the selection.

The default label Pie 1 will appear in the datasheet window.

Your slide should be similar to Figure 2-29.

FIGURE 2-29

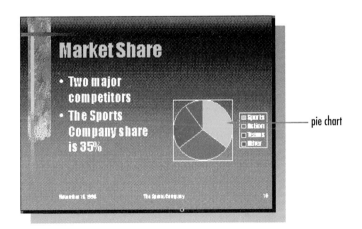

pie chart

The pie chart is inserted into the slide. Now that you have completed the slide, you would like to run the slide show.

■ Display slide 1, run the slide show, and view all the slides in the presentation.

Hiding Slides

Now that you have created the charts of sales growth and market share, you feel that the original slides showing the data are unnecessary. You decide to show only the charts during the presentation and to show the corresponding data slides only if requested. To do this you will hide the slides containing the data. You can hide slides in several views, but the procedure is easiest in Slide Sorter view.

■   Switch to ▦ Slide Sorter View.

Slide Sorter view also has its own toolbar, replacing the Formatting toolbar. While using this view, the buttons in the toolbar (identified below) help you perform many tasks.

> If the Slide Sorter toolbar is not displayed, select it from the toolbar Shortcut menu.

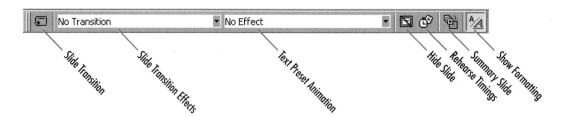

First you want to move slide 4 (with the data) to follow slide 5 (with the chart). Then you will hide the slide that contains the data.

> Drag the slide to move it.

■   Move slide 4 to follow slide 5.

> The menu equivalent is Sli**d**e Show/**H**ide Slide.

■   Click ▣ Hide Slide.

Notice that the slide number for slide 5 is surrounded by a box with a slash drawn through it. This indicates that the slide is hidden.

■   In a similar manner, reverse the order of slides 9 and 10 and hide slide 10.

You will run the slide show next to see how the hidden slides work.

■   Select slide 1 and run the slide show until the fourth slide (Sales Growth with area chart) is displayed.

Because the next slide, 5, is the hidden slide, it will not be displayed when you continue the slide show.

■   Display the next slide.

■   Continue the slide show until slide 9 (Market Share with chart) is displayed.

> The command to display a hidden slide is Go/Hidden Slide on the Shortcut menu. H is the keyboard shortcut.

The next slide is the hidden slide of Market Share data. To see the hidden slide,

■   Press H.

■   Continue the slide show until you are returned to Slide Sorter view.

Adding Transition Effects

Now that all the slides are created, you would like to use some of PowerPoint's special effects to enhance the on-screen presentation.

Concept 7: Special Effects

There are several special effects you can add to an on-screen presentation. Slide transitions, build slides, and animation are three commonly used special effects.

Transitions control how one slide moves off the screen and the next one appears. There are many different transition choices from which you can select. You may choose Dissolve for your title slide to give it an added flair. After that, you could use Wipe Right for all the slides until the next to the last and then use Dissolve again to end the show. As with any special effect, use slide transitions carefully.

Builds are used to display each bullet point, text, paragraph, or graphic independently of the other text or objects on the slide. You set up the way you want each element to appear (to fly in from the left, for instance) and whether you want the other elements already on the slide to dim or shimmer when a new element is added. For example, if your audience is used to reading from left to right, you could design your build slides so the bullet points fly in from the left. Then, when you want to emphasize a point, bring a bullet point in from the right. That change grabs the audience's attention.

Animation adds action to text and graphics so they move around on the screen. You can assign sounds to further enhance the effect.

When you present a slide show, the content of your presentation should take center stage. You want the special effects you use, such as builds, transitions, and animation, to help emphasize the main points in your presentation—not draw the audience's attention to the special effects.

The first enhancement you would like to make is to add a transition effect to the slides.

- ■ If necessary, select slide 1.

- ■ Click [⟲] Slide Transition.

The menu equivalent is Sli**d**e Show/Slide **T**ransition.

The Slide Transition dialog box on your screen should be similar to Figure 2-30.

FIGURE 2-30

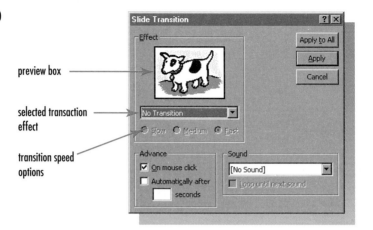

preview box ⟶

selected transaction effect ⟶

transition speed options ⟶

> You can vary the speed of each transition using the three-speed option.

■ Open the Effect drop-down list.

The Effect drop-down list box displays the names of the transition effects that can be used on the slides. Currently No Transition is selected. To see how a transition works, watch the preview box as you select the first effect, Blinds Horizontal.

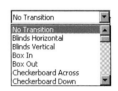

> Using ↑ and ↓ to move the highlight in the list box selects the effect and leaves the list open so you can preview others.

■ Press ↓.

■ Select a few of the other transition effects to see how they work.

You decide to try the Wipe Right transition effect on this slide.

> You can click the Preview box to watch the selected transition effect again when the Effect list is closed.

■ Select Wipe Right.

■ Click Apply.

Notice the 🔄 transition icon displayed below slide 1. This indicates that a transition effect has been applied to the slide. Also notice that the `Wipe Right` Slide Transition Effects button displays the name of the effect applied to the selected slide.

transition icon ⟶ 🔄   1

You feel this transition was not very noticeable, and instead decide to use the Random Transition effect, which will randomly select different transition effects to use. To select and change all the slides at once,

- ■ Choose Edit/Select All.

The keyboard shortcut is Ctrl + A.

- ■ Click [Wipe Right ▼] Slide Transition Effects.

Using the Slide Transition Effects button does not display the Slide Transition dialog box and it cannot be used to preview the effects.

- ■ Choose Random Transition (last option in drop-down list).

The transition icon now appears below each slide, indicating that a transition effect has been applied to all slides.

Adding Build Effects

The next effect you want to add to the slides is a build to progressively display each bullet on a slide. When a build is applied to a slide, the slide initially shows only the title. The bulleted text appears as the presentation proceeds. A build slide can also include different build transition effects, which are similar to slide transition effects. The effect is applied to the bulleted text as it is displayed on the slide.

You cannot preview build effects.

You would like to add a build to all slides in the presentation except slides 1, 4, and 9. Because all slides are still selected, you need to deselect the three slides only. To do this, hold down ⇧Shift while clicking on the slide.

- ■ Deselect slides 1, 4, and 9.

You can select and deselect multiple slides by holding down ⇧Shift while making your selection.

Now, to add a build to all the selected slides and use the Fly From Left build transition effect,

- ■ Click [No Effect ▼] Text Preset Animation.
- ■ Choose Fly From Left.

The ⠿ Build icon is displayed below the selected slides, indicating they are build slides. The Text Build Effects button shows the selected build effect.

Now that you have added the transition and build, you would like to see how they affect the slide show.

You can also use the Preset Animation and Custom Animation options on the Slide Show menu to add sound build effects. To use this option, you must be in Slide view.

- ■ Select slide 1 and run the slide show.

The first slide is displayed using a randomly selected transition effect.

- ■ Move to the next slide.

The second slide is displayed without the bulleted items. When a build is applied to a slide, the bulleted items are displayed only when you click or press Spacebar. This allows the presenter to focus the audience's attention and to control the pace of the presentation. The build effect displays the bulleted text using any one of the build transition effects. As you continue to display bulleted items, different build effects will be used.

- ■ To display the first bulleted item, click or press Spacebar.

Your screen should be similar to Figure 2-31.

FIGURE 2-31

first bulleted item ⎯⎯⎯

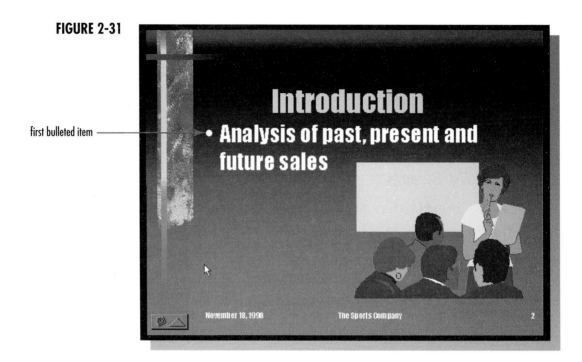

■ Click or press Spacebar until you have viewed the entire presentation.

You are returned to Slide Sorter view.

The last change you would like to make to the presentation is to add a final slide to mark the end.

■ Select slide 12 and insert a new slide using the ☐ Title Slide AutoLayout.

■ Switch to Slide view.

■ Enter the slide title **The Sports Company Market Analysis**

■ Reduce the point size of Market Analysis to 48.

■ Click ☰ Center.

■ Enter the slide subtitle text **The End**

■ Click ☰ Center.

■ Clear the selection.

Your screen should be similar to Figure 2-32.

FIGURE 2-32

The changes you made to the title master slide are reflected in the new title slide. The changes you made to this slide however, do not change the master.

Controlling the Slide Show

Now that you have made the layout changes to the presentation, you decide to run the slide show again from the beginning. If you were rehearsing the presentation, you could use the Rehearse Timings option on the Slide Show menu. It records the time you spend on each slide as you practice your narration. If your computer is set up with a microphone, you could even record your narration with the Record Narration option.

■ Move to slide 1 and start the slide show. View the first three slides.

Slide 4 should be displayed. As much as you would like to control a presentation, the presence of an audience usually causes the presentation to change course. PowerPoint has several ways you can control a slide show during the presentation. If someone has a question about a previous slide, you can go backward. For example,

■ Press Backspace.

You return the on-screen presentation to slide 3. But now, because the audience already viewed slide 4, you want to advance to slide 5. To go to a specific slide number, you type the slide number and press ←Enter.

■ Type **5**

■ Press ←Enter.

Slide 5 is displayed.

■ Display the four bulleted items.

> You also can select Previous from the shortcut menu or type P to go back a slide.

> You also can choose Go/Slide Navigator from the Shortcut menu to select a slide to move to.

Sometimes an audience member may get the entire presentation off track. If you find yourself on another topic altogether, you can black out the screen. To do this,

■ Press B.

You can also choose Screen/Black Screen from the Shortcut menu.

The screen goes to black while you address the topic. When you are ready to proceed with the presentation, to bring the slide back,

■ Press B.

Adding Freehand Annotations

During your presentation, you may want to point to an important word, underline an important point, or draw checkmarks next to items that you have covered. To do this you can use the mouse pointer during the presentation.

■ To display the mouse pointer, move the mouse pointer on the screen.

In its current shape, you can use the mouse pointer to point to items on the slide. You can also use it to draw on the screen by changing the pointer to a pen, which activates the freehand annotations feature.

You can also click the button that appears in the lower left corner of the slide when you move the mouse to open the Shortcut menu.

■ Right-click to display the Shortcut menu.

■ Choose Pen.

The keyboard shortcut is Ctrl + P.

The mouse pointer changes to a ⌀. To see how the freehand annotation feature works, you will underline the 1998 sales value. To draw, you drag the pen pointer in the direction you want to draw.

To draw a straight line, hold down ⇧Shift while dragging.

■ Move the mouse pointer under the $ in $10,200,000.

■ Drag the pen pointer until an underline is drawn.

Your screen should be similar to Figure 2-33.

FIGURE 2-33

underline   pen mouse pointer

■ Practice using the freehand annotator to draw any shapes you want on the slide.

You do not have to be concerned about cluttering your slides with freehand annotations because any freehand drawings are erased when you continue the presentation.

■ To turn off the freehand annotation feature, select Arrow from the Shortcut menu.

The mouse pointer shape returns to ⍟.

■ Continue running the slide show to view the rest of the presentation until you are returned to slide 1 in Slide view.

You can also erase annotations by selecting Screen/Erase Pen from the Shortcut menu. The keyboard shortcut is E.

The keyboard shortcut is Ctrl + A.

Creating Speaker Notes

When making your presentation, there are some critical points you want to be sure to discuss. To help you remember the important points, you can use speaker **notes pages**. These pages show a miniature of the slide and provide an area to enter notes. You can create notes pages for some or all of the slides in a presentation. Notes pages can also be used to remind you of hidden slides. You decide to create speaker notes for the charts in slides 4 and 9.

- Display slide 4.

The menu equivalent is **V**iew/**N**otes Page.

- Click  Notes Page View.

The top of the page displays the slide, and the lower part is a text box that is used to enter speaker notes.

- Click in the Notes text box.

Notice that the Font Size button shows the current font size is 12 points. To make the speaker notes easy to read in a dimly lit room while you are making the presentation, you would like to use a larger type size. While entering the text, you will also increase the screen magnification to make it easier to see the text as you type.

- Increase the font size to 24.

- Open the 28% Zoom control drop-down list.

The menu equivalent is **V**iew/**Z**oom.

- Select 75%.

- Type **1. The chart shows the growth in sales in millions of dollars.**

- Press ⏎Enter.

- Type **2. Sales increased from $5,100,000 in 1995 to $10,200,000 in 1998.**

- Press ⏎Enter.

- Type **3. Show the hidden slide next to see the sales data.**

Your screen should be similar to Figure 2-34.

FIGURE 2-34

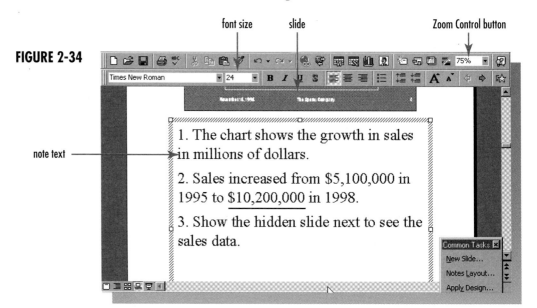

You would also like to add speaker notes for slide 9.

■ Move to Notes: 9 Market Share.

■ Select the notes text box and set the font size to 24.

■ Enter the following text for this notes page:

1. **Show the hidden slide next to see the data.**

2. **The Sports Company has been increasing steadily: 29% in 1995, 30% in 1996, 32% in 1997, and 35% in 1998.**

■ Set the zoom control to Fit and switch to Slide Sorter view.

Checking the Presentation

Before printing the presentation, you want to use the Style Checker to make a final check for typing errors and for visual clarity.

■ Choose **T**ools/St**y**le Checker.

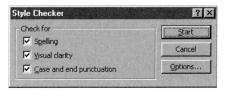

To see more details on what the Style Checker looks for,

■ Click  Options... .

To return all the options to their original default settings,

■ Click Defaults .

The Style Checker Options dialog box on your screen should be similar to Figure 2-35.

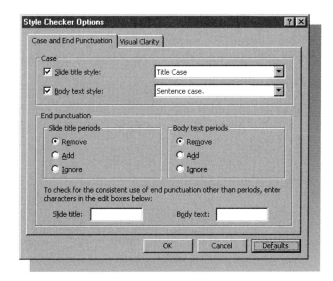

FIGURE 2-35

Notice that the default slide design uses Title Case (first letter of each word is capitalized) for slide titles and Sentence case (first letter of sentence is capital-

You move in Notes Page view just as in Slide view.

ized) for body text. No end punctuation is used. However, leaving the body text style option selected will change proper names to lowercase. To turn off this option,

■ Select Body text style.

■ Open the Visual Clarity tab.

Examine the Visual Clarity settings. The default settings use guidelines for proper slide design. The font size is large, the number of fonts used is small, and the amount of text on a slide is limited. All these settings help you adhere to good slide design. To run the style-check,

■ Click [OK].

■ Click [Start].

The Style Checker checks each slide in your presentation. If any words are misspelled, it stops so you can make the corrections.

■ Correct any words that are spelled incorrectly.

The Style Checker Summary dialog box shows that slide 6 exceeds the number of recommended bullets and slide 9 exceeds the recommended number of lines.

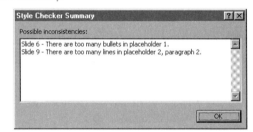

■ Click [OK].

■ Switch to Slide view and display slide 6.

This slide did not meet the visual clarity standards because there are seven bulleted items and the recommended maximum is six. The Visual Clarity settings are guidelines for good design. You can use your own judgment in deciding whether to change a slide or not. You feel this slide is acceptable.

■ View slide 9.

The last bullet in this slide contains three lines of text and the recommended maximum is two. Again, you feel this slide looks good.

■ Save the completed presentation file as Final Marketing Presentation.

Printing Selected Slides and Handouts

You have created both slides and notes pages for the presentation. To print the notes pages on which you entered text,

■ Choose File/Print/Print what/Notes Pages.

■ From the Print Range area, select Slides.

■ Type **4,9**

> The view you are in when saving the file is the view that will be displayed when the file is opened.

> If necessary, select the appropriate printer for your system.

> The comma is used to identify individual page numbers. If you wanted to print notes pages 4 through 9, you would use a hyphen to separate the page numbers.

- Click [OK].

The notes pages should be printing. Next you will print a few selected slides to be used as handouts.

- Choose **F**ile/**P**rint/Print **w**hat/Handouts (three slides per page).
- Select **S**lides.
- Type **1,2,4**

To scale the slides to fit the paper in your printer, and to add a thin border around the slides as a frame,

- Select Scale to Fit Paper.
- If necessary, select Fra**m**e Slides.
- Click [OK].
- If you are done working for the day, close the Common Tasks toolbar and exit PowerPoint.

> The Black & White print option is used to print colored slides on a black-and-white printer and is on by default.

LAB REVIEW

■ ■ ■ ■ ■ ■ ■ ■ ■ ■ ■

Key Terms

animation   (PR81)
attribute   (PR60)
AutoLayout   (PR70)
build   (PR81)
cell   (PR74)
chart   (PR73)
clip art   (PR66)
datasheet   (PR74)
design template   (PR54)
drawing object   (PR66)
graph   (PR73)
graphics   (PR66)
highlight   (PR74)
legend   (PR73)
master   (PR61)
notes page   (PR87)
picture   (PR66)
style   (PR60)
title   (PR73)
transition   (PR81)
X axis   (PR73)
Y axis   (PR73)

Command Summary

Command	Shortcut	Button	Action
View/**N**otes Page		🖳	Displays notes pages
View/**M**aster/**S**lide Master	⇧Shift + ⬚		Displays slide master for current presentation
View/**M**aster/**T**itle Master			Displays title master for current presentation
View/**Z**oom		28% ▾	Changes magnification of screen
Insert/**N**ew Slide	Ctrl + M	New Slide...	Inserts new slide
Insert/**P**icture/**C**lip Art		🖼	Inserts selected clip art on slide
Insert/**Ch**art		📊	Inserts chart
F**o**rmat/**F**ont/F**o**nt Style			Changes font style
F**o**rmat/Slide **L**ayout		Slide Layout...	Changes or creates a slide layout
F**o**rmat/Slide **C**olor Scheme			Changes color scheme of one or all slides in presentation
F**o**rmat/Appl**y** Design		Apply Design...	Changes appearance of slide by applying a different design template
F**o**rmat/Colors and Li**n**es		A ▾	Sets the line and fill color of selected object
Tools/St**y**le Checker			Checks spelling and slide design
Tools/E**x**pand Slide			Creates two slides out of one
Sli**d**e Show/**P**reset Animation		No Effect ▾	Adds build and animation effects
Sli**d**e Show/Slide **T**ransition		�	Adds transition effects
Sli**d**e Show/**H**ide Slide		🖾	Hides selected slide
Chart/**C**hart Type		📊 ▾	Changes chart type
Chart/Chart **O**ptions/Legend/**S**how Legend			Turns on/off display of legend

Matching

1. transitions	_____	**a.** shortcut for Select All command
2. Tools/Hide Slide	_____	**b.** the progressive display of one bulleted item at a time in a slide show
3. notes pages	_____	**c.** datasheet intersection of column and row
4. clip art	_____	**d.** hides selected slide
5. builds	_____	**e.** shortcut for Insert Slide command
6. Ctrl + A	_____	**f.** visual effects you see when you go from one slide to the next in a slide show
7. chart	_____	**g.** professionally drawn pictures
8. Ctrl + M	_____	**h.** predefined design settings for layout and colors
9. cell	_____	**i.** graphic representation of data
10. design template	_____	**j.** provides picture of slide and area for speaker notes

Hands-On Practice Exercises

Step by Step

Rating System
☆ Easy
☆☆ Moderate
☆☆☆ Difficult

☆
1. Damion is still working on his presentation on the proper way to prepare for a workout. He has had a larger sign-up for the presentation than expected and has scheduled a larger meeting room that is equipped with an on-screen projector system. He wants to make several changes to the presentation to take advantage of the new setup.

a. Open the presentation Workout created as Practice Exercise 1 in Lab 1. If necessary, switch to Slide view.

b. Change the design template to High Voltage. Select a color scheme and custom color for the background.

c. Use the title master to change the main title to Times New Roman, bold, 54 points. Change the subtitle to a point size of 40.

d. Clear the header and footer information from all slides. Add your name and the current date to the notes and handouts pages.

e. Add transitions and build effects of your choice to the slides. Run the slide show.

f. Switch to Notes Pages view. Move to note 7 and increase the font size of the note area to 24. Type the following note text:

Topic:	Fat Analysis
Date:	May 16
Time:	7:00 PM
Where:	Room 327 B

g. In Slide Sorter view, insert a new title slide at the end of the presentation for a closing slide. Add appropriate text and transition effects.

h. Check the presentation using the Style Checker; make any appropriate changes.

i. Run the slide show. Save the completed presentation as Workout Presentation.

j. Print the notes pages for slides 1 and 7. Close the presentation.

☆
2. Jason Ruskey, the promotions manager for Back-Road Bikes, wants to complete the presentation he will give to the outdoor clubs.

a. Open the presentation Back-Road Biking, created as Practice Exercise 2 in Lab 1. If necessary, switch to Slide view.

b. Change the template to Serene.

c. Change the title slide's subtitle to "Presented by [your name]."

d. Use the title master to change the font of the title slide to Ribbon 131 Bd BT and change the font size to 88. Change the subtitle to the font Ribbon 131 Bd BT, with a point size of 66. Change the text color to a color of your choice.

e. Use the slide master to change the title size to 54 and decrease the size of the second-level bullets to 24.

f. Clear the footer from all slides. Add your name and the current date to the notes and handout pages.

g. Add transitions and build effects of your choice to all the slides. Run the slide show.

h. Switch to Notes Pages view. Move to note 7 and increase the font size of the note area to 24. Type the following note text.

> *Mud and Muck—Tell funny story about sudden rain and hail storm last summer.*
>
> *Trail Dogs—Tell funny story about wild dog and partner's reaction.*

i. Insert a new title slide to the end of the presentation. Add appropriate text and transition effects.

j. Check the presentation using the Style Checker and make any appropriate changes.

k. Save the completed presentation as Back-Road Biking 2. Print the notes pages for slide 7. Print handouts (three per page) for slides 1, 7, and 10.

3. To complete the presentation for the Parks and Recreation Department on the building of three new pools, complete the following steps.

a. Open the presentation Pool Project, created as Practice Exercise 3 in Lab 1. If necessary, switch to Slide view.

b. Change the template to Whirlpool.

c. Change the font of the title on the title master to Caslon Openface BT. Change the text color to a color of your choice.

d. Insert a new slide after slide 6 using the Chart AutoLayout option. Increase the title font to 54. Enter the title "Money for Pools."

e. Create a pie chart using the information shown below. Clear the simple data in column D.

City	Fund Raising	Needed Funds
500000	400000	300000

f. Move the chart legend to the lower right corner of the chart area. Add a box with no fill around the chart.

g. Add a sun clip art image to slide 2 (or other appropriate image of your choice). Size the image and select a fill color.

h. Switch to Notes Pages view for slide 2. Increase the font size of the note text to 20 and enter the following text:

1. Park Central pool condemned.
2. City has experienced a 35% increase in pool usage.
3. Swimming program participation has increased by 55%.

i. Clear the footer information from all slides. Add your name and the current date to the notes and handouts pages.

j. Insert a new title slide to the end of the presentation. Add appropriate text.

k. Check the presentation using the Style Checker and make any appropriate changes.

l. Add transition and build effects of your choice to all the slides except slide 7. Hide slide 4. Run the slide show.

m. Save the completed presentation as New Pool Project. Print the notes pages for slides 2 and 7.

4. Karen Miller is ready to complete her presentation for the Future Workers of America Association.

a. Open the presentation Job Outlook, created as Practice Exercise 4 in Lab 1. If necessary, switch to Slide view.

b. Change the font of the title master to Wide Latin. Make the subtitle bold.

c. Change the font size of the bulleted items on slide 7 to 28 points.

d. Change the design template to Professional. Change the template colors to colors of your choice. Add the date to the handout pages.

e. On slide 2 insert the clip art titled Confused from the Cartoons category. Move and size the clip art appropriately.

f. On slide 3 insert the clip art Two Men Meeting at Desk from the People category. Move and size the clip art appropriately.

g. Move to slide 4. Insert a new slide using the Chart AutoLayout option. Enter the title "Hires through Recruiting 1996." Add a 3-D pie chart using the data shown below. Clear the sample data in columns C and D. Move the legend to the lower right corner of the chart area.

On-Campus	Off-Campus
73	27

h. Insert a new slide using the Chart AutoLayout option. Enter the title "Hires through Recruiting 1997." Add a 3-D pie chart using the data shown below. Move the legend to the lower right corner of the chart area.

On-Campus	Off-Campus
65	35

i. Insert a new title slide to the end of the presentation. Add appropriate text.

j. Add your name and the current date to the notes and handouts pages.

k. Add transition and build effects of your choice to all the slides except slides 1, 5, and 6. Hide the slides that contain the charts. Run the slide show.

l. Check the presentation using the Style Checker and make any appropriate changes.

m. Save the completed presentation as Job Hires. Print the handouts (three per page) for all the slides.

On Your Own

5. In this exercise you will complete the presentation for American Cruise Incorporated you started in Practice Exercise 5 of Lab 1.

Open the presentation Cruise Promotion. Enhance the appearance of the title slide. Select another design template. Include the company name American Cruise Inc. on the slides and handout pages. Add a clip art image of your choice to slides 2 and 3.

Insert a new slide as slide 6 using a layout for 60 pt bulleted text and a chart. Change the title of slide 6 to "Packages Sold" and make the font size 54. Enter the following bullets:

Bullet 1: 3rd Qtr sales declining
Bullet 2: 4th Qtr sales soaring

Add a chart to this slide using the data shown below.

	1st Qtr	2nd Qtr	3rd Qtr	4th Qtr
3 Day	234	200	78	356
5 Day	432	373	135	564
7 Day	346	290	164	432

Size the chart so the X-axis labels are displayed on two lines. Add a box with no fill around the chart.

Add transitions and build effects of your choice to all slides. Add a sound effect to slide 6. Include text on at least two notes pages. Save the completed presentation as Cruise Promotion 2. Print slide 6 and the two notes pages.

6. To complete this problem, you must have created the presentation in Practice Exercise 6 of Lab 1. You would like to improve the appearance and add interest to your presentation on managing your weight.

Open the presentation Weight Control. Enhance the presentation by changing the slide template, changing font styles and sizes, adding clip art, and applying builds and transitions.

Create notes pages for two of the slides. Add a header to the notes and handout pages that contain your name and the current date.

Print the notes pages. Save the presentation as Weight Control 2.

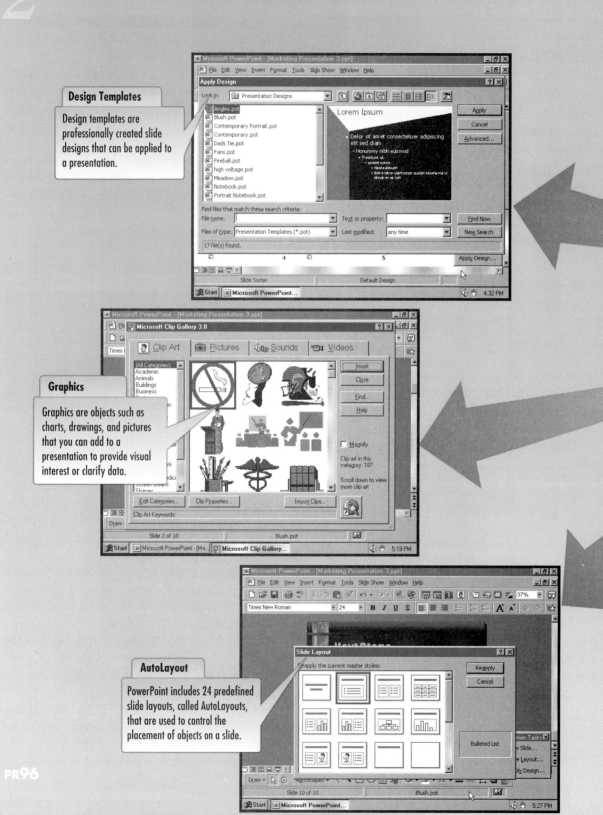

Design Templates

Design templates are professionally created slide designs that can be applied to a presentation.

Graphics

Graphics are objects such as charts, drawings, and pictures that you can add to a presentation to provide visual interest or clarify data.

AutoLayout

PowerPoint includes 24 predefined slide layouts, called AutoLayouts, that are used to control the placement of objects on a slide.

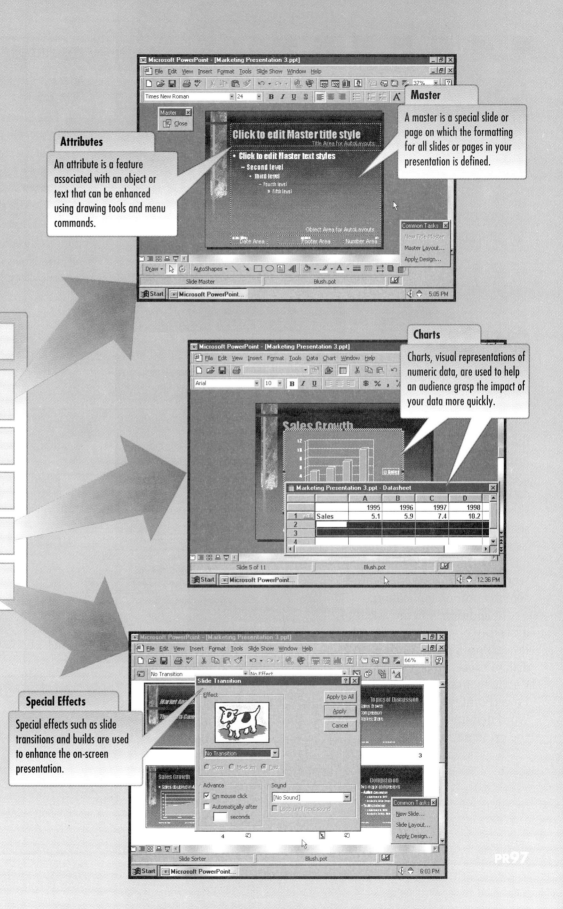

Concepts

Design Templates

Attributes
Master

Graphics

AutoLayout

Charts

Special Effects

Attributes

An attribute is a feature associated with an object or text that can be enhanced using drawing tools and menu commands.

Master

A master is a special slide or page on which the formatting for all slides or pages in your presentation is defined.

Charts

Charts, visual representations of numeric data, are used to help an audience grasp the impact of your data more quickly.

Special Effects

Special effects such as slide transitions and builds are used to enhance the on-screen presentation.

Sharing Information Between Applications

CASE STUDY

The Sports Company marketing manager reviewed the PowerPoint presentation you created and has asked you to include a chart created in Excel showing sales growth by product. Frequently you will find that you will want to include information that was created using a word processor, spreadsheet, or database application in your slide show. As you will see, it is easy to share information between applications, saving you both time and effort by eliminating the need to recreate information that is available in another application.

In addition, you are asked to distribute a copy of the PowerPoint presentation on a disk to those managers who are unable to attend the meeting. Because many of the managers are not familiar with PowerPoint, you have decided to embed the presentation in a Word document so you can provide instructions for running the presentation.

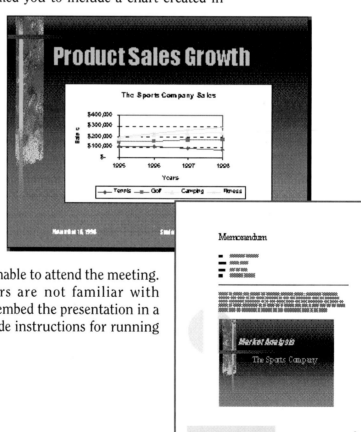

Concept Overview

The following concepts will be introduced in this lab:

1. Copy Between Applications	Information can be copied between applications and, if possible, inserted in the document in a format the application can edit.
2. Linked Object	Information that is copied from one file to another as a linked object maintains a connection between the two files, allowing the linked object to automatically update when the source file changes.
3. Embedded Object	Information that is copied as an embedded object to a destination file created by a different application becomes part of the file and can be updated by opening the object server from within the document in which it is inserted.

Copying Between Applications

First you will modify the PowerPoint presentation to include the graph showing sales by product. You have also decided to include a hidden slide with the actual product sales data. You have revised the presentation to include these new slides.

> This lab assumes that you are familiar with the Excel 97 program and how to chart data.

■ Load PowerPoint 97.

■ Open the file Marketing Presentation 4.

■ Scroll the window to see slides 6 and 7.

Your screen should be similar to Figure 3-1.

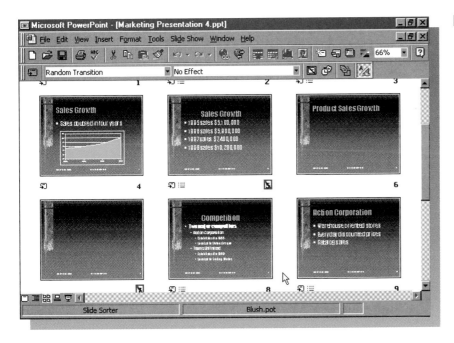

FIGURE 3-1

Slide 6 will display the chart, and slide 7, which is the hidden slide, will display the worksheet data. First you will copy the sales data from the Excel 97 file Product Sales to slide 7.

■ Display slide 7 in Slide view.

■ Load Excel 97 and open the file Product Sales on your data disk.

Your screen should be similar to Figure 3-2.

FIGURE 3-2

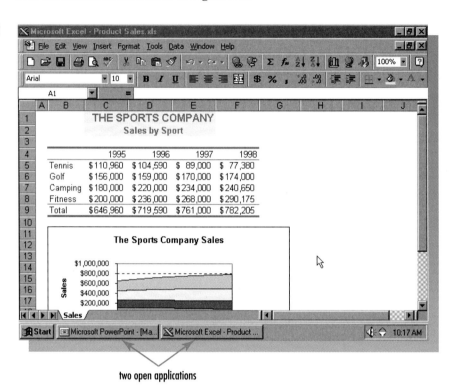

two open applications

The worksheet contains sales data by sport and an area chart of the data. There are now two open applications, PowerPoint and Excel. To make it easier to work with two applications, you will tile the windows to view both on the screen at the same time.

> **Right-click the taskbar and select Tile Vertically from the Shortcut menu.**

> **Click anywhere on the application window to switch between applications.**

■ Tile the two application windows vertically.

■ Select the spreadsheet data in cells B1 through F9.

■ Click 📋 Copy.

■ Switch to the PowerPoint window.

■ Choose Edit/Paste Special.

The Paste Special dialog box on your screen should be similar to Figure 3-3.

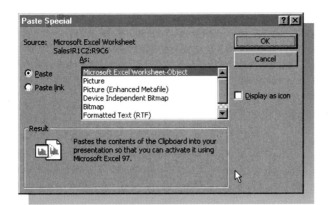

FIGURE 3-3

From the dialog box, you need to specify how you want the selection inserted into the slide. You want to paste the selection as a picture in PowerPoint.

> You will use many of these dialog box options throughout this lab.

Concept 1: Copy Between Applications

While using the Microsoft applications, you have learned how to use cut, copy, and paste to move or copy information within the same document and between documents in the same application. You can perform these same operations between applications. For example, you can copy a graph from an Excel worksheet and paste it into a PowerPoint presentation. Likewise, you can copy a PowerPoint presentation, or even a single slide, into a Word document. The information is pasted in a format that the application can edit, if possible.

From the As list box,

- Select Picture.
- Click [OK].
- Maximize the PowerPoint application window.
- Size and move the worksheet picture object appropriately.
- Change the background fill of the object to white so the data is easier to see.
- Deselect the object.

> Use the [⬛] Fill Color button to change the background.

Your screen should be similar to Figure 3-4.

FIGURE 3-4

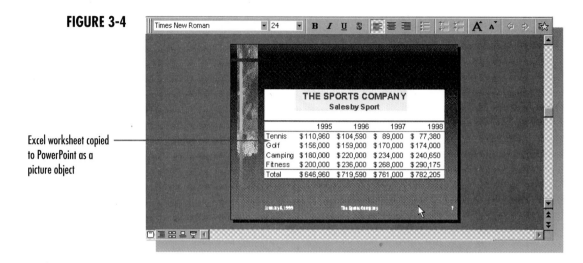

Excel worksheet copied to PowerPoint as a picture object

The worksheet is inserted into the slide as a picture object that can be manipulated from within PowerPoint using the Picture toolbar. Since you do not expect the sales data to change, this is acceptable.

Linking an Excel Chart to a PowerPoint Presentation

Next you will copy the area chart into slide 6 of the PowerPoint presentation.

- Restore the PowerPoint application window to its previous size.
- Display slide 6 in Slide view.
- Select the area chart.
- Switch to the Excel window and select the area chart.
- Click 🖻 Copy.
- Switch to the PowerPoint window.

Because you anticipate you may want to change the chart type, you will paste the chart object into the presentation as a linked object.

Concept 2: Linked Object

Information created in one application can also be copied into a document created in another application as a **linked object**. When an object is linked, the data is stored in the **source file** (the file it was created in). A graphic representation or picture of the data is displayed in the **destination file** (the document in which the object is inserted). A connection between the information in the source file and the destination file is established by the creation of a link. The link contains references to the location of the source file and to the selection within the document that is linked to the destination file.

When changes are made to the source file that affect the linked object, the changes are reflected automatically in the destination file while it is open. Otherwise the link is updated when the destination file is first opened. This is called a **live link**. When you create linked objects, the date and time on your machine should be accurate so that when you open the destination file, the program refers to the date of the source file to determine whether updates are needed.

- Select Edit/Paste Special/Paste Link/ OK .

- Appropriately size and center the linked object on the slide.

- Deselect the object.

Your screen should be similar to Figure 3-5.

The object type of Microsoft Excel Chart Object is already appropriately selected in the As list box.

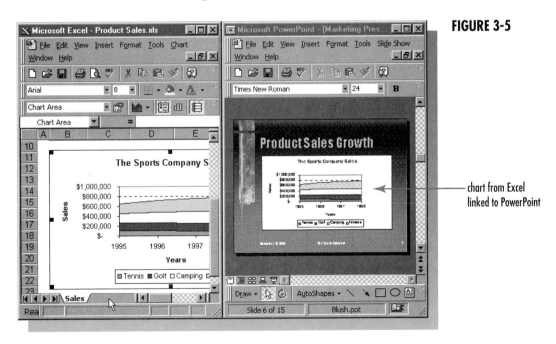

FIGURE 3-5

chart from Excel linked to PowerPoint

Because the chart is a linked object, if you change the data upon which this chart is based or make changes to the chart in Excel, the changes will be reflected in the chart in the slide. To see how this works, you will change the chart type to a line chart in Excel.

- Switch to the Excel window and, if necessary, select the chart.

- Open the ■ Chart Type drop-down list.

- Click ⟨⟩ Line Chart.

Your screen should be similar to Figure 3-6.

FIGURE 3-6

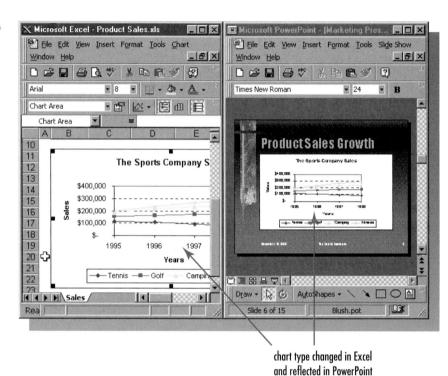

chart type changed in Excel
and reflected in PowerPoint

The chart changes to a line chart in Excel, and the change is automatically reflected in the linked chart in PowerPoint.

> If your chart did not update automatically, switch to PowerPoint, choose **E**dit/Lin**k**s and select the linked object, click ⟨Update Now⟩ to update it.

- Untile the application windows.

- Modify the slide footer to display your name and the current date on all slides except the title slide.

- Print the two new slides only.

- Update the file properties, save the PowerPoint presentation as Linked Marketing Presentation, and exit PowerPoint.

- Save the workbook file using the same file name and exit Excel.

Embedding a Presentation in a Word Document

Now that the PowerPoint presentation is complete, you will include a copy of the PowerPoint presentation in a Word memo for those managers who cannot attend the meeting. The memo to the managers has already been created.

- ■ Load Word 97.

- ■ To see the memo, open the file Marketing Presentation Memo.

- ■ If necessary, maximize the application and document windows.

Your screen should be similar to Figure 3-7.

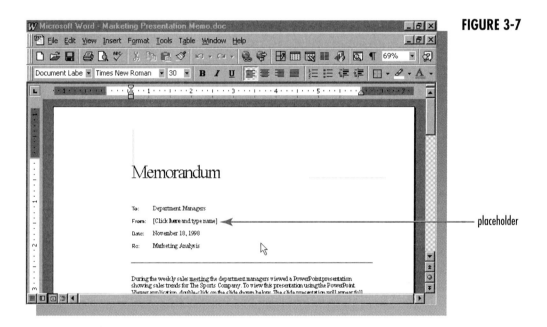

FIGURE 3-7

placeholder

- ■ Replace the placeholder with your name following "From:" in the memo heading.

- ■ If necessary, select the date and press F9 to update the date to display the current date.

Now you are ready to copy the presentation into the memo. You will copy it as an embedded object.

Concept 3: Embedded Object

Information can also be inserted into another application document as an **embedded object**. An object that is embedded is stored in the destination file and becomes part of the document. The entire file, not just an image of the selection that is displayed in the destination file, is stored. This makes a file containing an embedded object much larger than a file containing the same object using linking.

If the user has access to the application that created the embedded object, called the **server**, the embedded object can be edited or updated from within the destination file. The connection to the server is established through the use of a field code that identifies the server associated with the embedded object. Double-clicking on the embedded object starts the server application within the destination file. Any changes you make to the embedded object are not reflected in the original source file.

Object Linking and Embedding, or **OLE**, is the program integration technology that makes it possible to share data between applications. All Office 97 programs support OLE.

You should include PowerPoint Viewer on the disk with the memo for distribution to the managers.

Use **I**nsert/**O**bject in PowerPoint to link or embed an entire file.

By embedding the presentation, those managers who do not have a full version of PowerPoint can view the presentation using PowerPoint Viewer. PowerPoint Viewer is a separate application included with PowerPoint that can be distributed freely to others. It allows users to view presentations only.

■ Move to the blank line below the memo text.

■ Choose **I**nsert/**O**bject.

The Object dialog box is displayed. This dialog box is used to insert a new object or existing object into the current document. You will insert the contents of an existing presentation file into the memo.

■ Open the Create From File tab.

The Object dialog box on your screen should be similar to Figure 3-8.

FIGURE 3-8

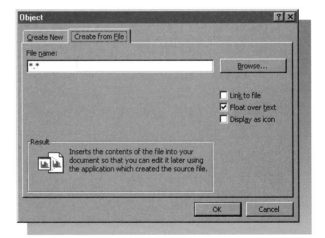

- Click [Browse...].

- From the Look In drop-down list box, select the appropriate drive for your system.

- Select Linked Marketing Presentation.

- Click [OK].

The file name appears in the File Name text box. If you choose [OK], you will embed the object. You can also link the object by selecting the Link To File option or display the embedded object as an icon by selecting the Display As Icon option. Whether you choose to link or embed the object, using this command places the entire contents of the source file into the destination file. If you want to place only selected pieces of text or graphics, use Copy and then Edit/Paste Special/Paste Link to link the selection, or Edit/Paste Special/Paste to embed the selection.

Since you will be distributing the memo on a disk, you cannot link the presentation because the readers will not have access to the source file. Therefore, you want to embed the presentation in the document. You also do not want to embed it as an icon, because you want the title slide to display in the printed copy of the memo to entice the reader to run the onscreen presentation.

> You also can open PowerPoint, use Edit/Select All to select all slides, use Edit/Copy or [ ] to copy the slides to the Clipboard, and then use Edit/Paste Special to embed the selection into the memo.

- Click [OK].

After a few moments, the first slide of the presentation appears in the memo.

> It may take a moment for the slide to appear in the document.

- Change the zoom setting to Whole Page.

- Center the slide on the page below the paragraph.

- Clear the selection.

Your screen should be similar to Figure 3-9.

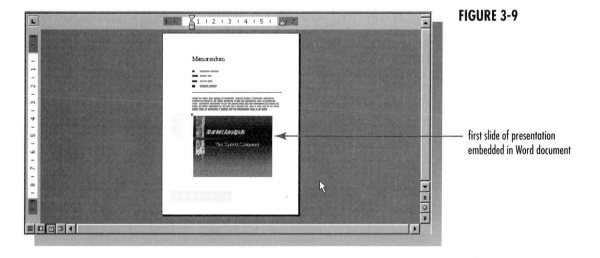

FIGURE 3-9

first slide of presentation embedded in Word document

Running the Slide Show from Word

Now that the presentation is embedded in the memo, you can view it from within Word.

■   Double-click on the slide.

PowerPoint is loaded or, if the full version of PowerPoint is not available, the PowerPoint Viewer application is loaded. The first slide of the presentation is displayed.

> You can cancel the slide show by pressing [Esc].

■   Continue running the slide show to view the rest of the slides in the presentation.

After viewing the last slide, you are returned to the Word document.

Editing an Embedded Object

If you are using the full version of PowerPoint to view the presentation in Word, you can also edit the presentation from within Word. As you are running the slide show, you decide to add your work phone number extension to slide 2 in case the managers want to ask a question about the materials. To edit the embedded presentation,

> Use Edit/Object/Edit in PowerPoint to edit embedded objects.

■   If necessary, select the presentation object.

■   Choose Edit/Presentation Object/Edit.

A warning box appears asking you if you want to update the links in the presentation. Since you linked an Excel chart in the presentation, you want to update the link in case any information was changed. To do this,

■   Click [OK].

After a few moments, the first slide appears in an editing border, and the PowerPoint application menu and toolbars are displayed.

■   Increase the Zoom to 50%.

Your screen should be similar to Figure 3-10.

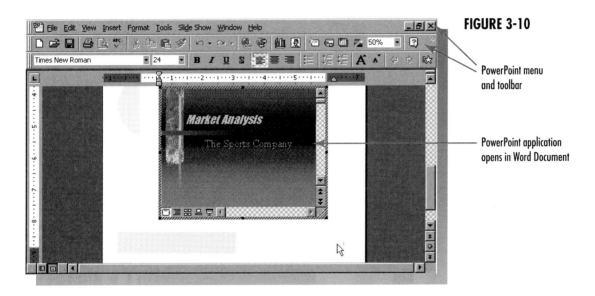

FIGURE 3-10

PowerPoint menu
and toolbar

PowerPoint application
opens in Word Document

- Display slide 2 and replace Student Name with your name.
- Add a demoted bullet below your name to display "-ext. 5264".

Breaking a Link

You also decide you do not want the presentation to be linked to the Excel file
containing the chart, because you do not plan to include a copy of the Excel file
with the memo document file that you will be giving to the managers. To break
the link between the files,

- Choose Edit/Links.

The dialog box is used to modify settings associated with linked objects. It displays paths and settings for all links in the document in the list box.

- Select the link in the list box.

The Links dialog box on your screen should be similar to Figure 3-11.

linked object

FIGURE 3-11

information about
selected linked object —

manually updates link
used to edit source file
changes object link path

deletes object link

used to specify how
a link is updated

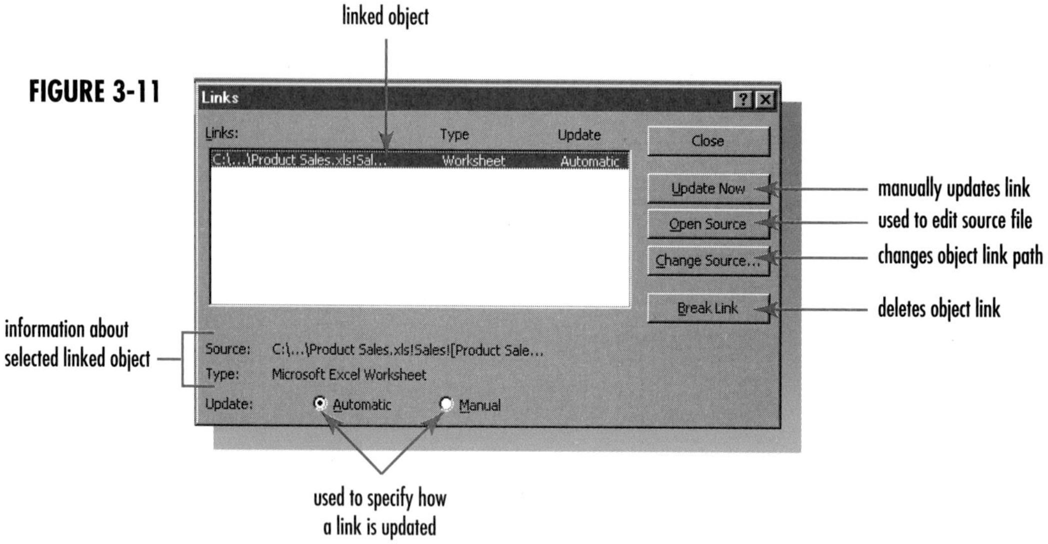

Now, below the list box, file information about the selected link is displayed.

The two update settings, Automatic and Manual, are used to change how a link is updated. Automatic, the default, updates the link whenever the file is opened. However, if a file contains many links, updating can take a lot of time. In a situation like this, you may want to change a link to update only when you specify using the [Update Now] button. The [Open Source] button will open the source file for the selected link. The [Change Source...] button allows you to modify the path to the source file if you move the source file to another location. Finally, the [Break Link] option deletes the object link field code, thereby breaking the connection between the source and destination files.

■ Click [Break Link].

The object is removed from the Links list box.

■ Click [Close].

The chart that you inserted into the presentation as a linked object is no longer linked to the copy of the presentation embedded in the memo. It is simply a pasted object. If any changes are made to the data or chart in Excel, the slide in this version of the presentation will not be updated. The chart is just a picture in the embedded presentation. However, the link still exists between the original presentation and Excel.

■ Clear the selection.

Before you save the file and copy it for distribution to the managers, you need to set the view as you want it to appear when the managers open the file.

■ Change the zoom to 75%. Move to the top of the document.

■ Update the file properties and save the document as Embedded Marketing Presentation Memo.

■ Exit Word.

Deciding When to Use Linking or Embedding

Most documents will not include both linked and embedded objects because the reasons for using each are different.

Use linking when:	Use embedding when:
File size is important.	File size is not important.
Users have access to the source file and application.	Users have access to the application, but not to the source files.
The information is updated frequently.	The data changes infrequently.

LAB REVIEW
■ ■ ■ ■ ■ ■ ■ ■ ■ ■ ■

Key Terms

destination file   (PR103)
embedded object   (PR106)
linked object   (PR103)
live link   (PR103)
Object Linking and Embedding (OLE)   (PR106)
server   (PR106)
source file   (PR103)

Command Summary

Command	Action
Edit/Paste **S**pecial/Paste **L**ink/**A**s/<object type>	Links a selection
Edit/Paste **S**pecial/**P**aste/**A**s/<object type>	Embeds a selection
Edit/Lin**k**s/**U**pdate Now	Updates selected linked object immediately
Edit/Lin**k**s/**B**reak Link	Breaks link to an object
Edit/**O**bject/**E**dit	Edits an embedded object
Insert/**O**bject	Links or embeds an entire file

Matching

1. linked object   _____   **a.** document in which object is inserted

2. source file   _____   **b.** application that created embedded document

3. embedded object   _____   **c.** object is represented in destination file and connected to source

4. destination file   _____   **d.** object is stored in destination file

5. server   _____   **e.** file in which object was created

Hands-On Practice Exercises

Step by Step

Rating System	
☆	Easy
☆☆	Moderate
☆☆☆	Difficult

1. To complete this problem, you must have completed Practice Exercise 2 in Lab 2 and created the file Back-Road Biking 2. Jason wants to send a memo to the Pacific Coast Outdoor Club, where he will be making a presentation the next week.

a. Add the following memo in a new Word document.

TO: Pacific Coast Outdoor Club

FROM: [Your Name]

DATE: [Current date]

Subject: Promotional demonstration for Back-Road Bikes

Thank you for your interest in Back-Road Bikes. At our presentation to your club next week, we will be using a PowerPoint slide presentation. To preview the presentation, simply load the Word document Back-Road Promo from the enclosed disk and double-click on the slide. You must have the PowerPoint Viewer program on your computer to view the slides. This program is also on the enclosed disk.

b. Embed the Back-Road Biking 2 presentation below the memo.

c. Save the Word document as Back-Road Promo. Print the document. Close the file.

2. To complete this problem, you must have completed Practice Exercise 3 in Lab 2 and created the file New Pool Project. You want to write a memo that will include the Pool presentation for people to view at home.

a. Embed the New Pool Project presentation you created into a new Word document based on the Elegant memo template.

b. Add the following memo above the embedded slide presentation:

TO:	All Concerned Citizens
FROM:	Student Name
DATE:	Current date
Subject:	Informational material for new pool construction

Thank you for your interest in your community's commitment to improving the services offered at your local parks. At our community presentation, we used a PowerPoint slide presentation. If you missed this presentation, you can view the presentation on your IBM computer at home. Ask the receptionist for a disk containing the necessary files. Then simply load the Word document New Pool Info from the disk and double-click on the slide. You must have the PowerPoint Viewer program on your computer to view the slides. This program is also on the disk.

c. Remove the cc line from the memo heading and save the Word document as New Pool Info. Print the document. Close the file.

3. To complete this problem, you must have completed Practice Exercise 4 in Lab 2 and created the file Job Hires. After Karen's presentation, she decides to send a memo to the Dean of Students about her concerns regarding on-campus recruiting.

a. Link slides 5 and 6 to a new Word document based on the Contemporary memo template.

b. Add the following memo above the linked slides:

TO:	Dean of Students
FROM:	Future Workers of America Association
DATE:	[Current date]
Subject:	Recruiting concern

It has been brought to our attention that on-campus recruiting is on the decline. We are forming a task force to address this situation head-on. With your support and guidance, we hope to reverse the downward trend.

c. If necessary, size the slides to fit on page 1.

d. Create a page break below the slides. Enter the following text on the new page:

As you can see from the following chart, the downward trend has been steady over the last few years.

e. Open the Excel document Recruiting. Create a column chart from the worksheet. Link the chart on the second page of the memo.

f. Karen rechecked the data for the chart and found that the data for 1995 should be 84 for on-campus and 17 for off-campus. Adjust the figures for 1995.

g. Break the link for the chart.

h. Save the Word document as Recruiting Alert Memo. Print the document. Close the file.

PRESENTATION

On Your Own

4. To complete this problem, you must have completed Practice Exercise 5 in Lab 2 and created the file Cruise Promotion 2. You want to create a one-page brochure about the cruise packages.

In a new Word document, enter:

American Cruises, Inc.
Plan your vacation today.

Format the text appropriately for the brochure. Link the Cruise Promotion 2 presentation you created below the text. Change the link to a Manual update. Return to the original presentation and add the bullet "Track increased requests for information" to slide 7. Manually update the brochure.

Save the Word document as Cruises On-screen Brochure. Print the document. Close the file.

5. In this problem you will complete the presentation you started in Practice Exercise 7 of Lab 1 for a class you are taking. Add transitions, builds, charts, and clip art that is appropriate for the presentation. Select a new template for the presentation. Add notes pages to slides that need reminders.

Create a link in your presentation to an Excel worksheet or chart. Embed the presentation you completed in a memo that introduces the presentation. Save the presentation and print the slides, notes pages, and handouts.

Save and print the memo.

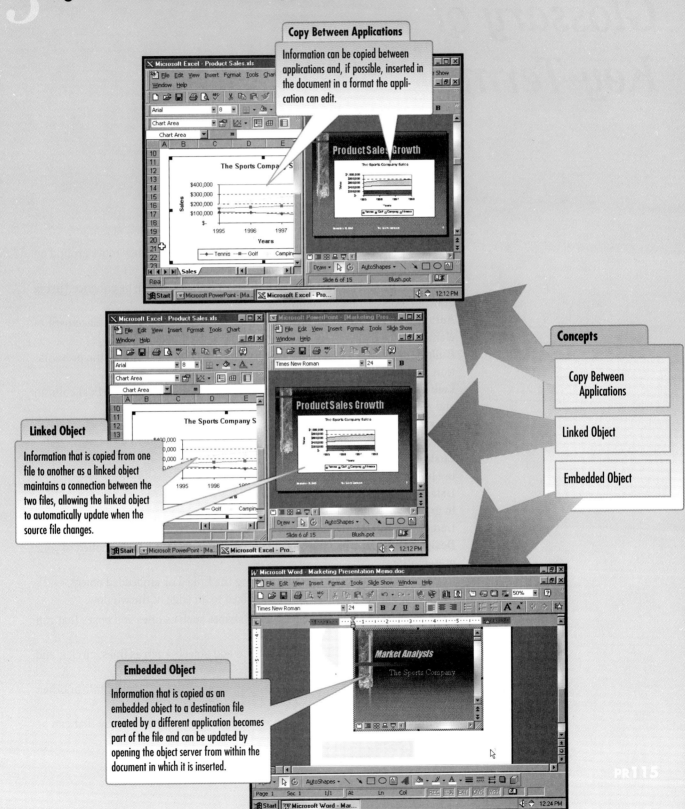

Copy Between Applications

Information can be copied between applications and, if possible, inserted in the document in a format the application can edit.

Concepts

Copy Between Applications

Linked Object

Embedded Object

Linked Object

Information that is copied from one file to another as a linked object maintains a connection between the two files, allowing the linked object to automatically update when the source file changes.

Embedded Object

Information that is copied as an embedded object to a destination file created by a different application becomes part of the file and can be updated by opening the object server from within the document in which it is inserted.

Glossary of Key Terms

Animation: Effect that adds action to text and graphics so they move around on the screen.

Attribute: A feature associated with an object or text that can be enhanced using drawing tools and menu commands.

AutoLayout: A predefined slide layout that is used to control the placement of elements on a slide.

Builds: An effect that progressively displays the bulleted items as the presentation proceeds.

Cell: The space on a datasheet created by the intersection of a vertical column and a horizontal row.

Chart: A visual representation of data.

Clip art: Professionally drawn images.

Custom dictionary: A dictionary you can create to hold words you commonly use but that are not included in the dictionary that is supplied with the program.

Datasheet: Table consisting of rows and columns holding data used to enter data to graph.

Demote: To move a topic down one level in the outline hierarchy.

Design template: Professionally created slide design that can be applied to your presentation.

Destination file: The document receiving the linked or embedded object.

Docked: A toolbar or menu bar that is fixed to an edge of the window.

Drawing object: An object consisting of shapes such as lines and boxes that can be created using the Drawing toolbar.

Drawing toolbar: A toolbar that is used to add objects such as lines, circles, and boxes.

Embedded object: An object created in one application and copied into another. It is stored in the destination file and edited using the screen.

Floating: A toolbar or menu bar that appears in a separate window that can be moved by dragging.

Font: A set of characters with a specific design.

Font size: Height of a character measured in points.

Footer: Text or graphics that appear on the bottom of each slide.

Formatting toolbar: A toolbar that contains buttons used to modify text.

Graph: *See* Chart.

Graphics: Non-text elements, such as charts, drawings, pictures, and scanned photographs, in a slide.

Handouts: Printed output that displays two or more slides on a page with space for audience members to make notes.

Highlight: Border surrounding the selected cell in a datasheet.

Legend: A brief description of the symbols used in a chart.

Linked object: An object that is created in a source file and linked to a destination file. Edits made to the source file are automatically reflected in the destination file.

Live link: A link that automatically updates the linked object whenever changes are made to it in the source file.

Main dictionary: Dictionary that comes with the PowerPoint 97 program.

Master: A special slide on which the formatting of all slides in a presentation is defined.

Move handle: Used to move menu bars and toolbars to a new location.

Notes page: Printed output that shows a miniature of the slide and provides an area for speaker notes.

Object: An item on a slide that can be selected and modified.

Object Linking and Embedding (OLE): The program integration technology that makes it possible to share data between applications.

Office Assistant: Used to get help on features specific to the Office application you are using.

Outline toolbar: Displayed in Outline view, it is used to modify the presentation outline.

Picture: An illustration created by combining lines, arcs, circles, and other shapes.

Placeholder: Box that is designed to contain objects such as the slide title, bulleted text, charts, tables, and pictures.

Point: A unit of type measurement. One point equals about 1/72 inch.

Promote: To move a topic up one level in the outline hierarchy.

Sans serif font: A font that does not have a flair at the base of each letter, such as Arial or Helvetica.

Selection rectangle: Hashed border that surrounds a selected placeholder.

Serif font: A font that has a flair at the base of each letter, such as Roman or Times New Roman.

Server: The application used to modify an embedded object.

Sizing handles: Small boxes surrounding selected objects that are used to change the size of the object.

Slide: An individual page of the presentation.

Slide show: Used to practice or to present the presentation. It displays each slide in final form.

Source file: The document in which the linked object was created.

Standard toolbar: A toolbar that contains buttons that give quick access to the most frequently used program features.

Style: Refers to the attributes, such as bold and italics, that can be applied to text.

Title: Text added to a chart to describe the data.

Transition: An effect that controls how a slide moves off the screen and the next one appears.

View: A way of looking at the presentation. Five views are available in PowerPoint.

Work area: Large area of the window where the presentation is displayed.

X axis: The horizontal axis of a chart.

Y axis: The vertical axis of a chart.

Command Summary

Command	Shortcut	Toolbar	Action
File/**N**ew	Ctrl + N	▯	Creates new presentation
File/**O**pen	Ctrl + O	▣	Opens selected presentation
File/**C**lose		✕	Closes presentation
File/**S**ave	Ctrl + S	🖫	Saves presentation
File/Save **A**s			Saves presentation using new file name
File/**P**rint	Ctrl + P	🖨	Prints presentation using default print settings
File/Proper**ti**es			Displays statistics and enters information about the presentation
File/E**x**it			Exits PowerPoint program
Edit/Paste **S**pecial/Paste **L**ink/**A**s/<object type>			Links a selection
Edit/Paste **S**pecial/**P**aste/**A**s/<object type>			Embeds a selection
Edit/**D**elete Slide	Delete		Deletes selected slide
Edit/Select A**l**l	Ctrl + A		Selects all slides
Edit/Lin**k**s/**U**pdate Now			Updates selected linked object immediately
Edit/Lin**k**s/**B**reak Link			Breaks link to an object
Edit/**O**bject/**E**dit			Edits an embedded object
View/**S**lide		▢	Switches to Slide view
View/**O**utline		▤	Switches to Outline view
View/Sli**d**e Sorter		▦	Switches to Slide Sorter view
View/**N**otes Page		▣	Displays notes pages
View/Slide Sho**w**		▣	Runs slide show
View/**M**aster/**S**lide Master	⇧ Shift + ▢		Displays slide master for current presentation

PR119

Command	Shortcut	Toolbar	Action
View/**M**aster/**T**itle Master			Displays title master for current presentation
View/**B**lack and White		[icon]	Displays slides in black and white
View/Slide M**i**niature			Displays or hides a slide miniature of current slide
View/**H**eader and Footer			Specifies information that appears as headers and footers on slides, notes, outlines, and handout pages
View/**Z**oom		28%	Changes magnification of screen
Insert/**N**ew Slide	Ctrl + M	New Slide...	Inserts new slide
Insert/**P**icture/**C**lip Art		[icon]	Inserts selected clip art on slide
Insert/**C**hart		[icon]	Inserts graph
Insert/**O**bject			Links or embeds a file
F**o**rmat/**F**ont/**F**ont		Times New Roman	Changes font typeface
F**o**rmat/**F**ont/**S**ize		24	Changes size of font
F**o**rmat/**F**ont/F**o**nt Style			Changes font style
F**o**rmat/Slide **L**ayout			Changes or creates a slide layout
F**o**rmat/Slide **C**olor Scheme			Changes color scheme of one or all slides in presentation
F**o**rmat/Appl**y** Design		Apply Design...	Changes appearance of slide by applying a different design template
F**o**rmat/Colors and Li**n**es		[icon] A ▾	Set the line and fill color of selected object
Chart/**C**hart Type		[icon] ▾	Changes chart type
Tools/**S**pelling	F7	[icon] ABC	Spell-checks presentation
Tools/St**y**le Checker			Checks spelling and slide design
Tools/E**x**pand Slide			Creates two slides out of one
Slide Show/**P**reset Animation/ **C**ustom Animation		No Effect	Adds build and animation effects
Slide Show/Slide **T**ransition		[icon]	Adds transition effects
Slide Show/**H**ide Slide		[icon]	Hides selected slide

Index

Appendix A

Additional PowerPoint 97 Features

- Create a presentation from an existing presentation
- Find and replace text
- Import text from Word
- Apply a template from another presentation
- Modify a sequence in Outline view
- Draw, rotate, and fill an object
- Add sound and movies
- Change tabs
- Add scanned images (pictures)
- Create a custom background
- Add an organizational chart
- Add a table
- Add links to other slides within the presentation
- Set automatic slide timing
- Electronically incorporate meeting feedback
- Export to overheads and 35 mm slides
- Present with Presentation Conferencing
- Save for Internet

■   Save for use on another computer.

■   Export an outline to Word.

Create a Presentation from an Existing Presentation

Many times it is faster to create a new presentation from an existing presentation. You can do this easily by modifying the existing presentation to meet the requirements of the new presentation and then saving the revised presentation using a new file name. You will change the Marketing Presentation to a Sales Presentation.

■   Open Marketing Presentation 4.

■   In slide sorter view, delete slide 3. Then delete slides 5 through 12.

Your screen should be similar to Figure A-1. The presentation now consists of six slides whose content is directly related to sales.

FIGURE A-1

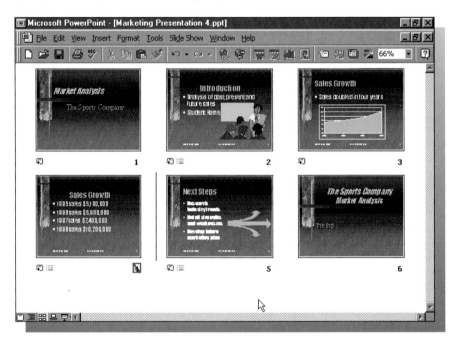

Find and Replace Text

You can also highlight text to restrict the search to the selection.

Next you want to edit the presentation by replacing the title text Market Analysis with the new presentation title, Sales Analysis. To do this quickly, you will use the Find and Replace feature to find the text you specify and automatically replace it with other text.

- Move to slide 1 and switch to Slide view.

- Choose Edit/Replace.

The Replace dialog box should be similar to Figure A-2.

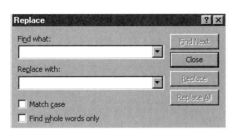

FIGURE A-2

The keyboard shortcut is [Ctrl]+H.

The Edit/Find command locates specified text only.

In the Find what text box, you enter the text you want to locate. The two options described in the table below allow you to refine how the search for the text you want to locate is conducted.

Option	Effect on Text
Match Case	Distinguishes between uppercase and lowercase characters. When selected, it finds only those instances in which the capitalization matches the text you typed in the Find what box.
Find Whole Words Only	Distinguishes between whole and partial words. When selected, it locates matches that are whole words and not part of a larger word. Finds cat only and not catastrophe too, for example.

The text you want to replace is entered in the Replace with text box. The replacement text must be entered exactly as you want it to appear in your document. You want to find all occurrences of the complete word "market" and replace them with the word "Sales." To enter the text to find and replace and begin the search,

- Type **market** in the Find what text box.

- Type **Sales** in the Replace with text box.

- Select Find Whole Words Only.

- Click [Find Next].

- If necessary, move the dialog box so you can see the located text.

After entering the text to find, do not press [↵Enter] or this will choose [Find Next] and the search will begin.

Immediately, the first occurrence of text in the presentation that matches the entry in the Find what text box is located and highlighted.

Your screen should be similar to Figure A-3.

located word

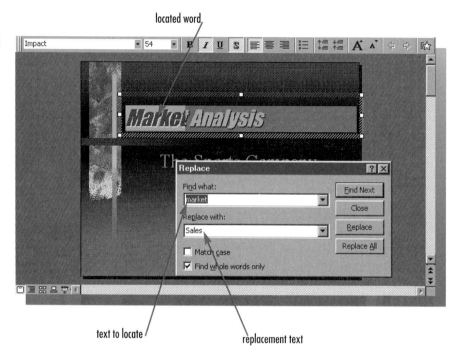

text to locate

replacement text

To replace the located word with the replacement text,

■   Click   Replace   .

The highlighted text is replaced and the search immediately continues. The next occurrence of the Find text is located.

■   Replace this occurrence.

The third occurrence of matching text is located in the notes pages.

■   In a same manner, replace this occurrence.

If you are changing all the occurrences it is much faster to use the Replace All command button. Exercise care when using Replace All, because the search text you specify might be part of another word and you may accidentally replace text you want to keep.

When using the Find command you can close the dialog box and use the ▲ and ▼ to find the previous or next occurrence of the text.

A message is displayed advising you that the search is complete. To close the message box,

- ■ Click [OK].
- ■ Close the Replace dialog box.
- ■ Switch back to Slide view.
- ■ Fix the title in the closing slide so that "Sales Analysis" is on the second line.
- ■ Replace Student Name in slide 2 with your name.

Now you are ready to save the presentation using a new file name.

- ■ Choose File/Save As.
- ■ Specify the location of your data disk (A:) as the location to save the file.
- ■ Enter the file name **Sales Analysis.**
- ■ Click [Save].
- ■ Print handouts (3 slides per page).
- ■ Close the Sales Analysis presentation.

Import Text from Word

The next presentation you are working on is for the new employee orientation meeting that is held each month. You have created a document in Word of topics to be used in this presentation and want to use this document as the basis of your presentation. To do this, you can import text created in other programs into PowerPoint to create a new presentation or to add slides to an existing presentation. PowerPoint determines the outline structure for the presentation from the heading styles in the imported document; Heading 1 style becomes a slide title, Heading 2 style becomes the first level of text, and so on. If the document does not contain heading styles, the paragraph indentations are used to create the outline. In plain text documents, tabs at the beginning of paragraphs define the outline structure. The document you will import has been formatted with Heading 1 and 2 styles.

- ■ Click [📂].
- ■ Choose All Outlines from the Files of Type drop-down list box.
- ■ Change the location to your data disk and select Orientation Agenda.rtf.
- ■ Click [Open].

> You can also use Insert/Slides from Outline to import text into an existing presentation.

Your screen should be similar to Figure A-4.

FIGURE A-4

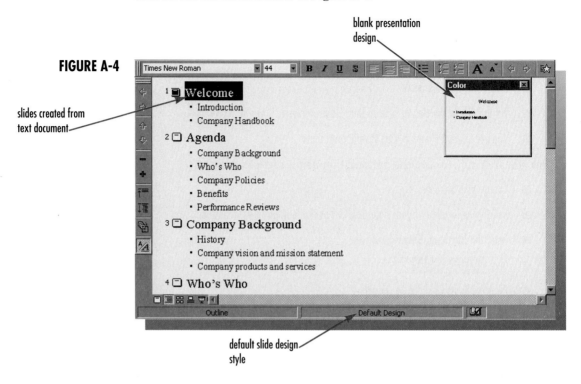

The new presentation created from the text file you imported is displayed in Outline view. Each Heading 1 style is the title for a new slide and each Heading 2 style appears as the text for the slide. The presentation uses the blank design style.

Apply a template from another presentation.

Next, you will apply the design used in the sales presentation to your new presentation.

- ■ Click 📄 .
- ■ If necessary, change the location to your data disk.
- ■ Change the file type to Presentations and Shows.
- ■ Select Sales Analysis.ppt.
- ■ Click   Apply   .

Your screen should be similar to Figure A-5.

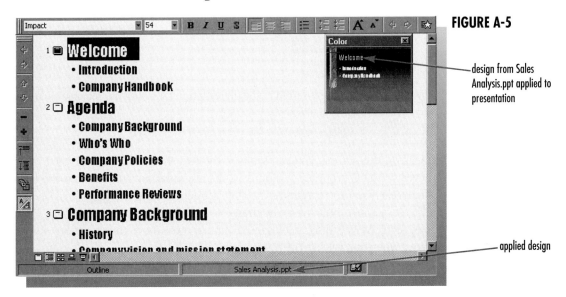

design from Sales Analysis.ppt applied to presentation

applied design

The design is applied to all slides in the presentation.

You also want to copy the title slide and the closing slide from the Sales Analysis presentation to the new employee orientation presentation.

- ■ Choose Insert/Slides From Files.
- ■ Click Browse... .
- ■ Select the Sales Analysis file.
- ■ Click Open .
- ■ Click Display .

The Slide Finder dialog box on your screen should be similar to Figure A-6.

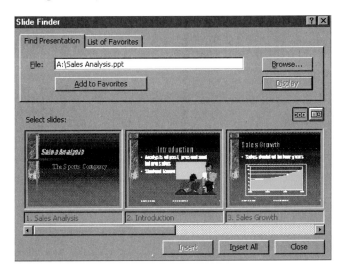

You can now select the slides you want to add to your presentation.

- ■ Select slides 1 and 6 in the presentation by clicking on them.
- ■ Click `Insert`.
- ■ Click `Close`.

The two new slides are inserted in the presentation following the selected slide (1).

Modify a Sequence in Outline View

Checking the outline, you can see that the two slides you inserted need to be moved to the appropriate locations in the presentation. Just like moving outline levels, you can reorganize the slide sequence using the ⬆ Move Up and ⬇ Move Down buttons or by dragging and dropping the slide icon. As you drag, a horizontal line shows where the selection will be placed when you release the mouse button.

- ■ The third slide icon and text are already selected. Drag the slide selection to the end of the presentation.
- ■ Click on the slide 2 icon to select it and drag it above the first slide icon.

Your screen should be similar to Figure A-7.

FIGURE A-7

slides rearranged in Outline view

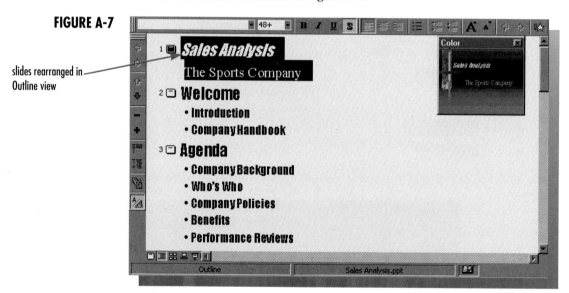

The slides are now in sequence in the correct order.

- ■ Use Find and Replace to change the title on the Title and End slides to New Employee Orientation.
- ■ Close the Replace dialog box.

Draw, Rotate, and Fill an Object

The next change you want to make is to add a drawing to the title slide to make it more interesting. You will include text in the object and enhance its appearance by adding a shadow, rotating the shape and filling it with a pattern.

- ■ Display the title slide in Slide view.
- ■ Display the Drawing toolbar.
- ■ Click AutoShapes ▾ and select <u>S</u>tars and Banners.
- ■ Click 🎀 Down Ribbon.
- ■ Click on the slide below the company name and drag to create the autoshape object.
- ■ If the shape is not visible, click 🖎 ▾ and select Automatic.

Your screen should be similar to Figure A-8.

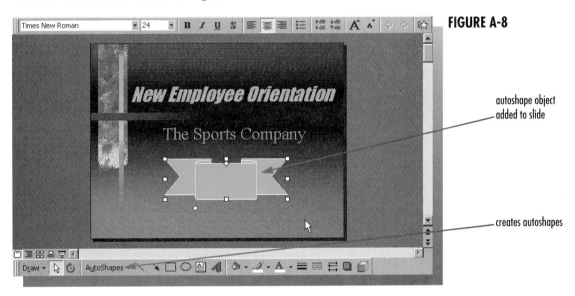

autoshape object added to slide

creates autoshapes

Next you will add text to the object and enhance its appearance using several features on the drawing toolbar.

- ■ Right-click on the autoshape object to open the Shortcut menu and select Add Te<u>x</u>t.
- ■ Change the font to Arial and bold.
- ■ Type **A Great Place to Work!**

- Click ▣ Shadow and select any shadow style from the pop-up menu.
- Click ▣ Shadow and select Shadow Settings.
- Use the Shadow Settings toolbar to enhance the appearance of the shadow by changing the shadow color to a color of your choice and nudging the shadow as needed.
- Close the Shadow Settings toolbar.
- Click ⟳ Rotate.
- Drag the rotate handle to change the angle of the shape.
- Click ⟳ Rotate again to turn off this feature.
- Click ⬧ ▾ Fill Color and choose Fill Effects.
- Select a color of your choice from the Texture tab of the Fill Effects dialog box.
- Size the shape appropriately.
- If necessary change the font color.

Your screen should be similar to Figure A-9.

> The rotate handles are small circles on each corner of the selected object.

FIGURE A-9

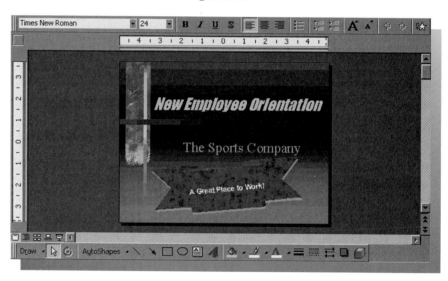

Add Sound and Movies

Sound and movies can be used to draw the audience's attention to a particular point or to liven up a slow presentation. By default, the sound or video starts when you click its icon during a slide show. PowerPoint also allows you to change the play settings to play the sound or video as soon as you move to the slide. You will add the Drum Roll sound clip to the Welcome slide to attract the audience's attention.

- Display slide 2 in Slide view.
- Choose Insert/Movies and Sounds/Sound from File.

The Insert Sound dialog box lists the sound files that are included with Office 97.

■   Double click Drumroll.wav.

A sound icon 🔊 appears on the slide. You can play the sound by clicking the sound icon during a slide show.

■   Move the sound icon to the bottom right corner of the slide.

■   Click 🖥 to run the slide show starting with the current slide.

■   Click the 🔊 sound icon.

If you have speakers you will hear the sound. Instead of clicking the sound icon to start a sound, you can change how you start a sound by positioning the mouse over the icon. In addition, you can add custom animation settings to a sound clip. You will change the settings so that the sound plays automatically before any other animation occurs on the slide.

■   Press [Esc] to return to Slide view.

■   Add a slide transition effect of your choice to this slide.

■   Choose Slide Show/Custom Animation.

■   From the Play Settings tab, select Play Using Animation Order.

■   Select Hide While Not Playing.

■   From the Timing tab, select Automatically.

■   Click [OK   ].

■   Start the slide show again from this slide to see how your changes affect the presentation.

The drum roll plays immediately following the slide transition.

Change Tabs

Next you will add a slide presenting a brief history of the company.

■   Insert a new slide after slide 4 using the Bulleted List layout.

■   In Slide view, add the slide title History.

■   Click in the text placeholder box.

■   Click ☰ to turn off bullets.

■   If necessary, display the ruler.

You will enter the list of dates and events shown on page A-13. To make it easier to align the two columns, you will set tab stops. A **tab stop** is a stopping point along a line to which text will indent when you press [Tab]. You can select from four different types of tab stops that control how characters are positioned or aligned with the tab stop. The four tab types, the alignment tab mark that appears on the ruler, and the effects on the text are explained in the following table.

Alignment	Tab Mark	How It Affects Text	Example
Left	⌊	Extends text to right from tab stop	left
Center	⊥	Aligns text centered on tab	center
Right	⌋	Extends text to left from tab stop	right
Decimal	⊥	Aligns text with decimal point	35.78

> The default tab type is Left.

Setting different types of tab stops is helpful for aligning text or numeric data vertically in columns. Using tab stops ensures that the text will indent to the same set location. Setting tab stops instead of pressing Tab or Spacebar repeatedly is a more professional way to format a document, and it's faster and more accurate.

You can quickly specify tab stop locations and types using the ruler. To select a tab stop type, click the tab alignment selector box on the left end of the ruler to cycle through the types. Then to specify where to place the selected tab stop type, click on the location in the ruler. Drag any tab marker to a new position or off the ruler to remove it. You will add a left tab stop at the 1 inch and 2.5 inch positions.

- Click the 1 position on the ruler.
- Click the 2.5 position on the ruler.
- Press Tab twice.
- Type **Year**
- Press Tab.
- Type **Event**
- Press ←Enter.

Your screen should be similar to Figure A-10.

FIGURE A-10

tab alignment selector box

text aligned at tab stops

left tab stops

- Set the font size to 32.

- Continue entering the information shown below. Remember to press ⌈Tab⌉ to create the columns.

    1948   Founded by Harvey Wilton
    1952   Built first store
    1976   Acquired 3 new stores
    1985   P. J. McCurdy, President
    1993   Expanded to 20 stores

Add Scanned Images

Next, you want to add a picture of Harvey Wilton to the history slide. You can use Insert/Picture/From Scanner to create a digital copy of a photograph using a scanner that is connected to your computer. Then the image can be edited using Microsoft Photo Editor and saved as a picture file. The picture file is then inserted into the slide just like any other graphic.

- Choose Insert/Picture/From File/Wilton.jpg.

- Click Insert .

> Microsoft Photo Editor must be installed to edit a scanned image.

After a picture is added to a slide, you can further edit it using features on the Picture toolbar. For example you can crop the picture, add special effects to it, and adjust its brightness, contrast, and color.

- Use the Picture toolbar features to crop and modify the picture as you like.

- Move and position the text and image on the slide as appropriate.

- Clear the selection.

Your screen should be similar to Figure A-11.

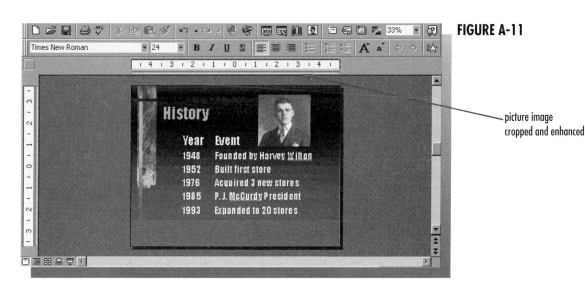

FIGURE A-11

picture image
cropped and enhanced

Create a Custom Background

Finally, because this slide contains a lot of information, you want to change the slide background of this slide only to a simple background design.

- Choose Format/Background.
- Open the color drop down list and select Fill Effects.
- Select a background of your choice from the Texture tab.
- Click OK.
- Select Omit background graphics from master.
- Click Preview to see how your selection will appear. If necessary, select a different texture color.
- Click Apply to only change current slide.
- Move and size the text placeholder box until it is centered on the slide.

This text uses the purple mesh texture

Your screen should be similar to Figure A-12.

FIGURE A-12

custom background
applied to slide

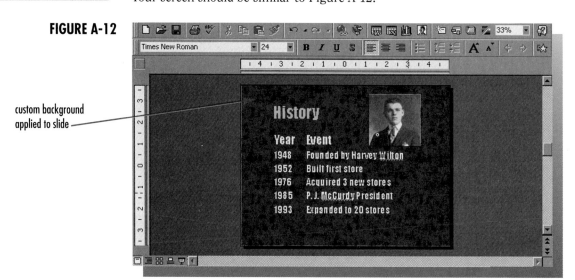

Add an Organizational Chart

The next slide you want to add to the presentation is a graphic representation of the organization of the company called an organizational chart.

You can also use Insert/Picture/Organization Chart to add this element to a slide.

- Insert a slide after slide 6 selecting the Organization Chart layout style.
- If necessary, switch to Slide view.

A placeholder for the organizational chart containing four boxes is displayed in the new slide.

- Add the title **Sports Company Organization** in a font size of 48.
- Double-click the organizational chart to activate it.

The Organization Chart window on your screen should be similar to Figure A-13.

FIGURE A-13

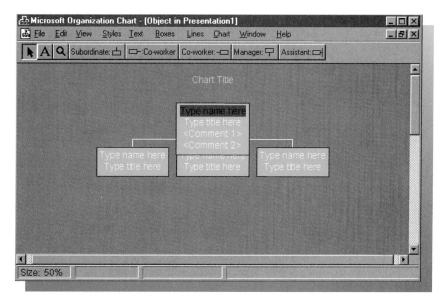

The chart is displayed in the Microsoft Organization Chart program window. The menu and toolbar are used to edit and enhance the appearance of the chart. You need to replace the placeholder labels in each box with the people's names and positions within the company. The top box is activated and ready for you to replace the placeholder text.

Use **H**elp/**I**ndex on the Organization Chart menu for further help on this feature.

- Enter the name **P. J. McCurdy** and the title **President.**

- Click in each of the other boxes to activate them and replace the placeholders with the following information:

David Stofka	Marsha Santori	Your Name
Vice President	Vice President	Vice President
Personnel	Finance	Add a title of your choice

- Enhance the appearance of the chart by adding features such as borders and shadows, and changing the color of the boxes and text to colors of your choice.

- Choose **F**ile/E**x**it and Return to Presentation.

- Click [**Yes**] to update the chart in the presentation.

- Size and position the organizational chart on the slide.

- Clear the selection.

Your screen should be similar to Figure A-14.

FIGURE A-14

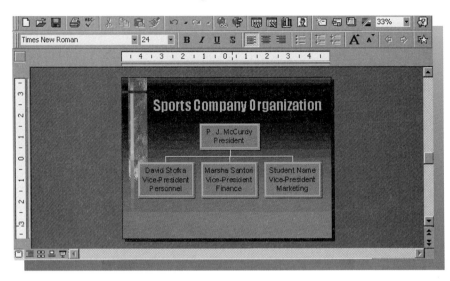

Add a Table

Next, you want to create a table to display information about vacation benefits (shown on page A-17). A table is made up of rows and columns of cells that you can fill with text and graphics. Tables are commonly used to align numbers in columns and then sort and perform calculations on them. They make it easier to read and understand numbers.

- Insert a new slide after slide 9 using the Table layout.

- Remove the title placeholder and drag the table placeholder up to cover the title space.

- Double-click the table placeholder.

- Specify 2 columns and 7 rows.

- Click OK .

Your screen should be similar to Figure A-15.

FIGURE A-15

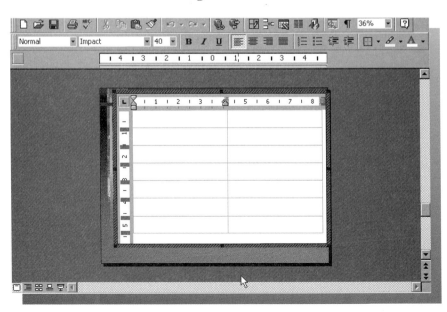

The table placeholder is enlarged so you can add text and modify the table using the menu and toolbar features. To add text, simply click in each cell and type. Use [Tab] to move to the next cell.

- ■ Drag to select row 1 and set the font size to 36 for the column headings.

- ■ Select rows 2 through 7 and set the font size to 28.

- ■ Add the information shown below to the table (see Figure A-16).

Length of Service	Annual Vacation Days
Less than 1 year	0
1 - 3 years	5
3 - 5 years	10
5 - 10 years	15
10 - 20 years	20
Over 20 years	30

Using the Table menu or Borders and Table toolbar buttons, modify the table as follows:

- ■ Set the Cell Height and Width to Auto (T**a**ble/Cell Height and **W**idth/AutoFit).

- ■ Center the text in all columns.

- ■ Change the font color of the table heading to bright green and all other cells to white.

- ■ Click outside the table window to return to the slide and adjust the size and placement of the table.

Your screen should be similar to Figure A-16.

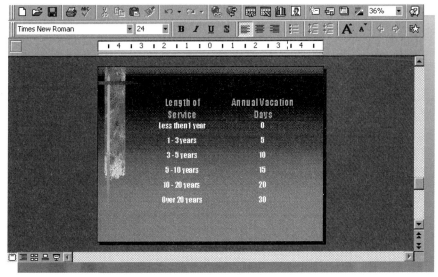

FIGURE A-16

- ■ Save the presentation as New Employee Orientation to your data disk.

Add Hyperlinks

The next addition to the presentation you want to make is to create hyperlinks between slides in the presentation. A **hyperlink,** also called a **hypertext link** or simply a **link,** is a connection to another slide in the presentation, to another presentation, to a Word document, or to an address on the Internet. Clicking on a link quickly displays the location associated with the requested link. You can create a hyperlink from any text or object, including a shape, table, or picture within a presentation. When you use a hyperlink within a presentation, you might want to consider creating a return hyperlink so you can quickly return to the original slide.

First you will create a hyperlink from the Agenda slide to the Company Background slide and then back to the Agenda slide.

■   Move to slide 3.

■   Highlight the "Company Background" text.

■   Click 🖳 Insert Hyperlink.

■   Click   Browse...   next to the Named Location in File text box.

■   Select "4. Company Background" from the Hyperlink to Slide dialog box.

■   Click   OK   .

■   Click   OK   .

> The menu equivalent is Insert/Hyperlink and the keyboard shortcut is [Ctrl]+K.

Your screen should be similar to Figure A-17.

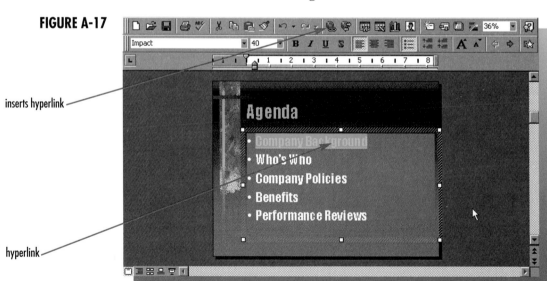

FIGURE A-17

inserts hyperlink

hyperlink

The hyperlink text appears underlined and in a color that coordinates with the color scheme you are using. To see how the hyperlink works,

■   Run the slide show from the current slide.

■   Click the Company Background hyperlink.

The Company Background slide is displayed. Next you will create a hyperlink back to the Agenda slide. You will add an action button to the slide and associate the hyperlink with the button.

- ■ Display slide 4 in Slide view.

- ■ Click AutoShapes ▾ on the Drawing toolbar and select Action Buttons.

- ■ Click 🎖 Return.

- ■ Drag to create the button shape on the bottom right corner of the slide.

The Action Settings dialog box on your screen should be similar to Figure A-18.

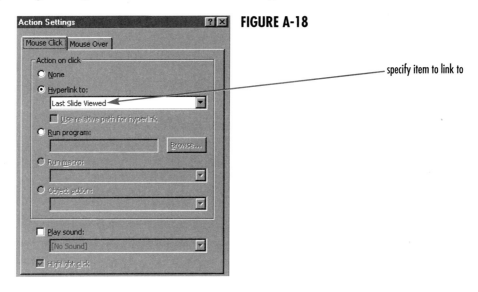

FIGURE A-18

specify item to link to

The tabs in this dialog box allow you to associate two actions with the object: clicking the hyperlink or holding the mouse over it to activate it. You can also set a hyperlink to play a sound when the mouse moves over an object and then click the object to jump to another slide. When you set up a hyperlink, it's best to select the mouse-click method. If you select the mouse-over method, it's possible to jump when you really don't want to.

Your next step is to associate the action that you want to occur with the button. In this case, you want to create a hyperlink to another slide in the presentation.

The menu equivalent is Sli**d**e Show/ Action Butt**o**ns.

- ■ From the Hyperlink To drop down list, select Slide.

- ■ From the Hyperlink to Slide dialog box, select 3. Agenda.

- ■ Click OK .

- ■ Click OK .

- ■ If the action button does not display, click 🖌 ▾ Fill Color and select Automatic.

Your screen should be similar to Figure A-19.

FIGURE A-19

action button

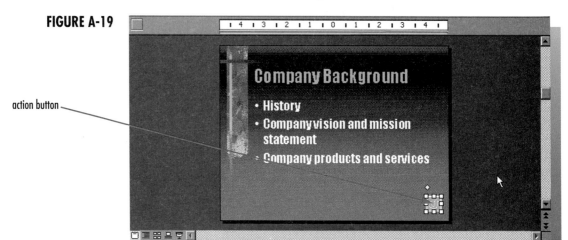

To see how the hyperlink works,

■ Run the slide show from the current slide.

■ Click the Action button.

The Agenda slide is displayed.

> You can use copy and paste to quickly copy the Action button from slide 4 to the other slides.

■ Return to Slide view and create hyperlinks on the Agenda slide to slides 6, 8, 9, and 11 and add Action button hyperlinks on each of these slides back to the Agenda slide.

■ Run the slide show again to test your hyperlinks.

Set Automatic Slide Timing

In addition to manually moving through a slide show, you can set the length of time a slide appears on the screen. To do this, you can set a time manually for each slide, and then run the slide show and view the timings you set. Another way is to use the rehearsal feature, where you can record timings automatically as you rehearse. You can also adjust the timings you've already set and then rehearse the new ones.

> Use Sli**d**e Show/**R**ehearse Timings to access the rehearsal feature.

First you will add a transition to all slides. Then you will manually set a length of time to display the first 3 slides.

■ Switch to Slide Sorter view and make slide 1 active.

■ Click 🔲 Slide Transition in the Slide Sorter toolbar.

■ Apply the Random Transition effect to all slides.

■ Select slides 1, 2, and 3.

■ Click 🔲 Slide Transition in the Slide Sorter toolbar.

■ In the Advance box, clear the **O**n Mouse Click option and select the Automati**c**ally After option.

■ Set the time to 5 seconds.

■ Click Apply .

Your screen should be similar to Figure A-20.

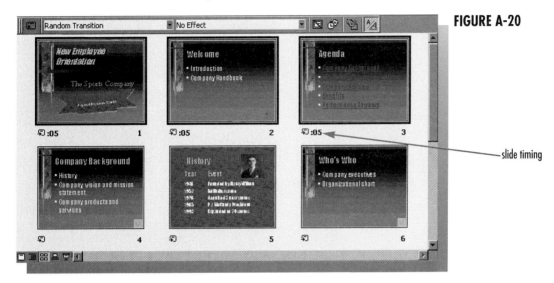

FIGURE A-20

slide timing

■ Run the slide show again to see how the timings work (remember to wait 5 seconds to allow the first 3 slides to advance automatically).

Electronically Incorporate Meeting Feedback

While you are running a presentation, you can take minutes, record action items, and add to notes pages using the Meeting Minder. You want to practice using this feature so you are comfortable using it during the real presentation. You will create a meeting note recording the date of the presentation and an action item to remind yourself to invite the Vice President of Personnel to attend the next new employee orientation.

■ Run the slide show from the beginning.

■ Right-click on the first slide and from the Shortcut menu select Meeting Minder.

■ In the Meeting Minutes text box type **September orientation meeting.**

■ In the Action Items tab, type **Invite VP Personnel** in the Description text box.

■ Type **your last name** in the Assigned To text box.

The Meeting Minder dialog box on your screen should be similar to Figure A-21.

FIGURE A-21

If you click on the slide you can continue running the presentation and the Meeting Minder dialog box remains open and ready for you to continue to record notes.

■ Click Add .

■ Click OK .

■ End the slide show and make slide 13 active in Slide Sorter view.

Action items appear on a new slide at the end of your slide show. You can also post the action items to Microsoft Outlook, or you can transfer the minutes and action items to a new Word document and then print that document.

■ Choose Tools/Meeting Minder.

■ Click Export... .

■ Select Send meeting minutes and action items to Microsoft Word.

■ Click Export Now .

Your screen should be similar to Figure A-22.

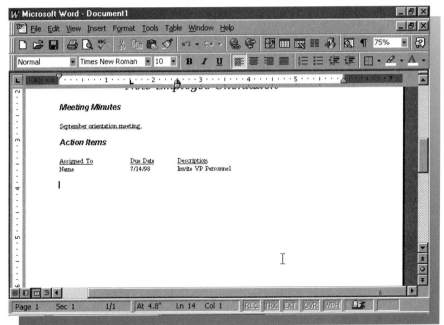

Word opens and the text from the meeting minutes and action items is entered into a new document.

- ■ Print the document.

- ■ Exit Word without saving the document.

- ■ Since you do not want slide 13 to be part of the final presentation, delete the slide.

Export to Overhead and 35mm Slides

As mentioned in Lab 1, you can also create a presentation for use with other types of output, such as overhead transparencies and 35mm slides. When planning a presentation it is always a good idea to choose the correct format for your presentation before you begin creating slides. Otherwise, slide layouts you create may not work with the output you plan to use. This is because the format settings you choose set the frame size for your slides. You want to see how your presentation would look if it were formatted for 35mm slides.

- ■ If necessary, switch to Slide Sorter view.

- ■ Choose **F**ile/Page Set**u**p/**S**lides sized for/35mm Slides.

The Page Setup dialog box should be similar to Figure A-23.

FIGURE A-23

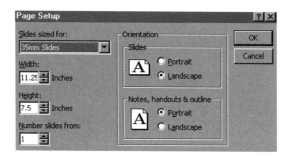

The height and width settings automatically change to reflect the size needed for 35mm slides. To see how this change effects your slides,

■ Click  .

Each slide is reformatted to the new size needed for 35mm slides. If you were to actually have 35mm slides made, you would check the slides to make sure all the information is fully displayed. In addition, you would remove the action buttons and the hypertext links from the slides. Finally, when your presentation is complete you can contact a service bureau that can make 35mm slides from the PowerPoint file. PowerPoint includes access to Genigraphics, a service bureau that can be used to prepare slides and other media from PowerPoint files. If you have installed the Genigraphics wizard, it can be used to help you prepare an electronic order and automatically transmit your file and order to Genigraphics for processing. To see how this feature works,

■ Choose **F**ile/Sen**d** To/**G**enigraphics.

■ Read the information in each step of the Genigraphics Wizard, clicking Next > to move through the steps. Click Cancel when the Shipping Instructions screen appears.

■ When you are done, return the format of the presentation to On-screen Show.

If the Genigraphics Wizard is not installed on your system this command will not be available.

Present with Presentation Conferencing

Over a network or the Internet you can make a presentation to participants in different locations at the same time using the Presentation Conference Wizard. If you are preparing a presentation for use with Presentation Conference the following elements of a presentation cannot be viewed or heard by the audience:

■ Multimedia objects such as sound or video clips except sound effects applied to transitions and animations if the audience's computers have the necessary hardware.

■ Embedded objects, such as a chart from Microsoft Excel.

■ Editing of linked or embedded objects.

Before using presentation conference, set up a conference call to exchange information such as the names of computers on which the audience will view the presentation or, if using the Internet, the address of the presentation. Then, both the presenter and participants use the Presentation Conference Wizard to guide them through the setup process.

Although you cannot actually run a presentation conference, you will use the Presentation Conference Wizard to see what questions are asked and what information you would need to provide before giving a presentation conference.

■ Choose **T**ools/**P**resentation Conference.

The Presentation Conference Wizard dialog box on your screen should be similar to Figure A-24.

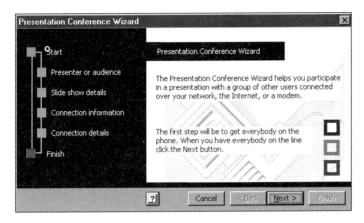

FIGURE A-24

■ Read the information in each step of the Presentation Conference Wizard, clicking Next > to move through the steps.

■ Click Cancel to end the wizard at the last step.

If you were actually a participant in a presentation conference you would need to click Finish before the presenter does, or you won't be connected. When the conference begins, the presentation appears on the screen.

As the presenter, you have access to all the tools that can normally be used to control a slide show such as the Slide Navigator and Slide Meter. You can also use the Meeting Minder without it appearing on the participants' computers. All conference participants can use the annotation pen to write and draw on the slides.

Save for Use on the Internet

If you want to publish a presentation on the Web, PowerPoint provides several online templates that help you design your presentation for online viewing. You can also save any existing presentation in HTML format for viewing on the Web. You would like to see how the New Employee Orientation presentation would look if it were converted for use on the Web.

■ Choose **F**ile/Save as **H**TML.

The Save As HTML Wizard dialog box on your screen should be similar to Figure A-25.

FIGURE A-25

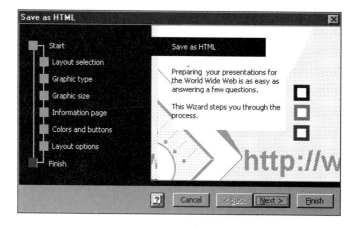

■ Read the instructions in the Save As HTML Wizard clicking   Next >   to move through the Wizard accepting the defaults for all options. When asked to save the file, specify your data disk as the location. When asked if you want to save the final settings, select Don't Save.

The presentation was quickly converted into a series of linked Web pages. To view the presentation on the Web you would need to open a browser program such as Netscape Navigator or Internet Explorer. If you have access to a browser complete the following steps.

■ Click 🌐 to open the Web toolbar.

■ In the address text box, enter **a:\Employee Orientation\sld001.htm**

Your browser program is opened and the first page of the presentation is displayed in the window.

You could also open your browser program and type the file name in the location text box.

■ Click the Forward button to move through the presentation.

■ When you are done, close your browser program.

■ Close the Web toolbar.

Save for Use on Another Computer

Often you may give a presentation in another location using a computer at that location. To make it easy to take your presentation with you, PowerPoint includes the Pack and Go Wizard. This wizard is used to compress and save a presentation across multiple disks. It also includes all linked documents and multimedia files that are used in the presentation. If the computer you will be using does not have PowerPoint installed, it also packages the PowerPoint Viewer on the disk. To see how the Pack and Go Wizard works, you will use it to copy the New Employee Orientation presentation.

- Choose File/Pack and Go.
- Follow the instructions in the Pack and Go Wizard. Do not include the viewer.

The files are compressed and saved to a file with a PPZ file extension. When you are ready to use the PowerPoint file on the other machine, you need to unpack the file first by running the Pngsetup.exe file that was created by the Pack and Go Wizard. You will also need to specify the location on the computer where you want to copy the presentation to.

Export an Outline to Word

Now that the text and organization of the New Employee Orientation presentation is nearly complete, you want to copy it to Word. You can then provide the speakers in the presentation with the outline to use as a guide to create the content of the additional support slides to include in the presentation.

- Choose File/Send To/Microsoft Word.

From the Write-Up dialog box you select the layout you want the presentation to appear in Word. The options allow you to position existing notes next to or below the slides, to include blank lines for additional notes, or to export just an outline of the presentation text without slide images. To export the outline only,

- Choose Outline Only.
- Click OK .

Your screen should be similar to Figure A-26.

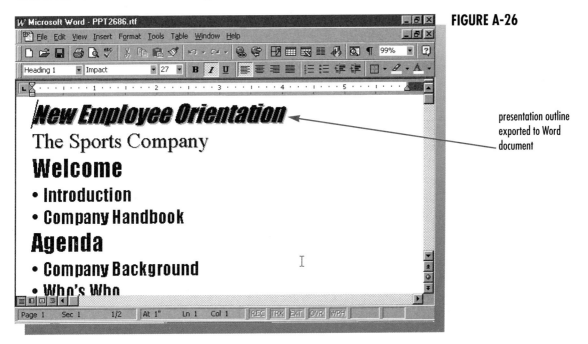

FIGURE A-26

presentation outline exported to Word document

Word is opened and a copy of the outline is exported from PowerPoint and imported into Word as a new document with a temporary file name.

■ Save the outline as Orientation Outline with a Word document file type (.doc) to your data disk.

■ Print the document.

■ Close Word.

■ Print handouts (3 slides per page) of the New Employee Orientation presentation.

■ Close the presentation.

■ Exit PowerPoint.

Key Terms

Hyperlink
Hypertext link
Link
Tab stop

Practice Exercises

1. Open the Job Outlook presentation you created in problem 4 of Lab 1. You are planning to write an article for a company newsletter and would like to use the presentation as an outline. Export the presentation to Word. Save the document as Job Outline. Print the outline.

2. To complete this problem you must have completed problem 3 of Lab 2. Now that construction of the swimming pools is almost complete you would like to create a new presentation to honor the staff and fundraisers. Open the Pool Outline.doc file in PowerPoint and apply the slide design from the New Pool Project presentation. Insert the first and last slide from the New Pool Project presentation into the new presentation. Use Find and Replace to change "Expanded" to "Increasing" in the presentation. Create hyperlinks to the slides on the Presentation Overview slide and Action buttons back to the Overview slide. Save the new presentation as Thank you Presentation. Print the slides six per page.

3. Open the Back-Road Biking 2 presentation you created in problem 2 of Lab 2. Add the Mountain.jpg picture to slide 2. Use the picture toolbar to modify the picture as necessary. Add a new slide after slide 9. Apply the Table slide layout. Enter the slide title "Attendance Projections." Create a table that contains the following:

Event	Maximum Capacity	Pre-registered
Day tours	50	35
Overnight trips	120	25
Races	300	175

Center the data in the capacity and pre-registered cells. Add a Callouts AutoShapes object of your choice to the Real Life Adventure slide (7). Add the text "Did you hear the one about" to the object. Appropriately size and color the object and text. Use the Rotate Object button to change where the callout points. Print slides 1, 2, 4, 7, and 10 as six per page. Save the presentation to your data disk.

4. Open the Cruise Promotion 2 presentation you created in problem 5 of Lab 2. You would like to modify the presentation to be given to new sales associates. Delete slide 4. Insert a new slide after slide 3 and apply the organizational chart layout. Add appropriate text to the organizational chart and include your name as one of the vice presidents. Apply a custom background to the organizational chart slide to make it unique. Add a new slide after slide 6 and apply the title slide layout. Create an end-of-presentation slide on the new slide. Add a drawing object of your choice to the slide. Use the features you learned to change the color, size and shape of the object. Use Pack and Go to compress the presentation for use on another machine. On a separate disk, save the presentation for Internet use and preview the presentation in you Internet browser. Print the slides six per page. Save the presentation as Cruise Associates.

5. Create an outline in Word for a presentation you plan on giving. Import the outline into PowerPoint. Apply the slide design from the Market Analysis Presentation to the outline. Add a sound transition to the second slide to draw the audience's attention. Insert a new slide where appropriate and create a table of data using custom set tabs. Use Meeting Minder to remind yourself of the things you need to do before the presentation. Practice your presentation with Rehearsal timings. Run the presentation and adjust the timings as necessary. Enhance the presentation as necessary and print the slides six per page.